A PLUME BOOK

SUCCESS BUILT TO LAST

JERRY PORAS coauthored (with Jim Collins) *Built to Last: Successful Habits of Visionary Companies,* which has sold over one million copies. He is Stanford Graduate School of Business Lane Professor of Organizational Behavior and Change, Emeritus, and lectures worldwide.

STEWART EMERY, considered one of the fathers of the Human Potential Movement, served as the first CEO of EST, cofounded Actualizations, and is the bestselling author of *Actualizations: You Don't Have to Rehearse to Be Yourself* and *The Owner's Manual for Life.* As a consultant, he asked questions that led MasterCard to its legendary "Priceless" campaign.

MARK THOMPSON is an executive coach, advisor to senior management teams, award-winning audio book producer, and former executive producer of Schwab.com. *Forbes* magazine listed him as one of America's top venture investors with the "Midas" touch.

Visit www.successbuilttolast.com.

Praise for *Success Built to Last*

"If we are to live in a world that works for everyone, we must create lives that matter. This book presents a path to the kind of lasting success that transcends fear and endows healthy self-esteem. This is a book for all of us who care about the future of all of us."

—Jack Canfield, bestselling author, Chicken Soup
for the Soul® series and *The Success Principles*™

"There is no greater thing you can do with your life and your work than follow your passions—in a way that serves the world and you. In this book you will learn from unknown and famous people—inspiring leaders like Nelson Mandela and entrepreneur Michael Dell, along with schoolteachers, scientists, community worker, athletes, artists, and the presidents of nations. Everyone wants success, but you can do better than that. This is an extraordinary book that finally reveals a meaningful 'secret formula' for success based on the lives of remarkable people."

—Sir Richard Branson, founder, Virgin Brands

"In business and in life, lasting success takes teamwork, integrity, and the courage to stick with what really matters. It's the best five players that win the game, not the five best players. That's what this book is all about."

—Richard Kovacevich, chairman, president, and CEO of Wells Fargo

"You can make a difference if you put your passions to work in a way that builds a better life for you, your business, and your community. *Success Built to Last* shows you how."

—Steve Forbes, editor in chief, *Forbes*

"Anything worth doing in life takes a team. If you want to create a life that matters—as you will see in this book—you've got to recruit a team to your dream."

—David Stern, commissioner, National Basketball Association

"There is nothing more important you can do than create a life that matters for you and your family. As a leader and a parent, you've got to read this book and then give it to the teens in your family!"   —Greg Foster, president, IMAX Films

"Want to pick the brains of successful, influential people? For your career's (and life's) sake, I hope you read *Success Built to Last* this weekend. For the world's sake, let's hope this is the most-read business book of the year."

—Keith Ferrazzi, CEO, Ferrazzi Greenlight and coauthor of the bestseller *Never Eat Alone*

"John Deere himself said, 'I will not put my name on a product that does not have the best in it that is in me.' Imagine using that same standard in your personal life and career. When you commit yourself to excellence that would make you proud to put your name on everything you do, then you will have *Success Built to Last.*"

      —Robert Lane, chairman and CEO, John Deere

"The best coaching you will ever get on creating a life that matters is in this book!"

  —Marshall Goldsmith, executive coach and author/coeditor of twenty-two books, including *The Leader of the Future* and *What Got You Here Won't Get You There*

"An incredible book and a must-read for anyone interested in achieving enduring success for themselves, their family, their stakeholders, and their community."

—Jason Jennings, bestselling author, *It's Not the Big That Eat the Small . . . It's the Fast That Eat the Slow; Less Is More;* and *Think Big, Act Small*

"In *Success Built to Last,* the authors show readers how to pursue their passions and achieve success beyond their wildest dreams, while staying true to who they are. The book is a 'must read'!"

      —Bill George, former chairman and CEO, Medtronic, and bestselling author, *Authentic Leadership*

"You will find rich insights about how to make a life—not just a living."

      —Barry Z. Posner, dean and professor of leadership, Santa Clara University, and bestselling coauthor, *The Leadership Challenge* and *A Leader's Legacy*

"The book is both moving and practical. It also reflects the personal experiences of the authors—three leaders whom I admire and respect. As far as I'm aware, this is the most thoroughly researched work on enduring success and leadership available. The ideas are amazingly accessible."

—Spencer Clark III, chief learning officer, Cadence Design Systems

"In the end, whether or not your business prospers or fails is all a matter of how you behave and the decisions that you take. It is up to you. Let this exceptional book be your servant and guide."

—Lord Alistair McAlpine, treasurer, British Conservative Party, 1975–1990

"If you're crazy enough to do what you love for a living, then you're bound to create a life that matters. *Success Built to Last* wisely counsels you to go nuts about something meaningful. That's what you're here to do, for heaven's sake."

—Herb Kelleher, chairman and cofounder, Southwest Airlines

"At last, a powerful new resource for leaders struggling to create a life that matters, a guide book for the journey to greater significance for leaders across the sectors and around the world."

—Frances Hesselbein, chairman and founding president, Leader to Leader Institute (formerly the Peter F. Drucker Foundation)

SUCCESS BUILT TO LAST

Creating a Life That Matters

Jerry Porras
Stewart Emery
Mark Thompson

A PLUME BOOK

PLUME
Published by Penguin Group
Penguin Group (USA) Inc., 375 Hudson Street, New York, New York 10014, USA •
Penguin Group (Canada), 90 Eglinton Avenue East, Suite 700, Toronto, Ontario
M4P 2Y3, Canada (a division of Pearson Penguin Canada Inc.) • Penguin Books
Ltd., 80 Strand, London WC2R 0RL, England • Penguin Ireland, 25 St. Stephen's
Green, Dublin 2, Ireland (a division of Penguin Books Ltd.) • Penguin Group
(Australia), 250 Camberwell Road, Camberwell, Victoria 3124, Australia (a division
of Pearson Australia Group Pty. Ltd.) • Penguin Books India Pvt. Ltd., 11
Community Centre, Panchsheel Park, New Delhi – 110 017, India • Penguin Group
(NZ), 67 Apollo Drive, Rosedale, North Shore 0745, Auckland, New Zealand (a
division of Pearson New Zealand Ltd.) • Penguin Books (South Africa) (Pty.) Ltd.,
24 Sturdee Avenue, Rosebank, Johannesburg 2196, South Africa

Penguin Books Ltd., Registered Offices: 80 Strand, London WC2R 0RL, England

Published by Plume, a member of Penguin Group (USA) Inc. This is an authorized
reprint of a hardcover edition published by Wharton School Publishing. For information address Pearson Education, Inc., Upper Saddle River, NJ 07458.

First Plume Printing, September 2007
10   9   8   7   6   5   4   3

The Library of Congress has catalogued the Wharton School Publishing edition as
follows:
Porras, Jerry I.
  Success built to last : creating a life that matters / Jerry Porras,
Stewart Emery, Mark Thompson.
    p. cm.
  ISBN 0-13-228751-X (hc.)
  ISBN 978-0-452-28870-6 (pbk.)
  1. Success in business. 2. Successful people. I. Emery,
Stewart, 1941–   II. Thompson, Mark, 1957–   III. Title.
  HF5386.P757 2006
  650.1—dc22

                            2006013081

Printed in the United States of America

To Rick Porras, Vanessa Thompson, and Paul Emery—
all on their way to creating a life that matters

CONTENTS

*greatness at the intersection of pain and passion * Don't make the future pay the debts of the past * Beyond blame—creating a future that matters*

PART III: ACTIONSTYLES—TURNING PASSION
INTO ACTION

Chapter 9: Earning Your Luck—Preparing for Serendipity by Using Big Hairy Audacious Goals * *Why you have to earn your luck * The myth of authenticity * How big, hairy, audacious goals help you prepare for serendipity * Too much presidential information * Bold risks measured in small steps * When bad goals happen to good people * The secret life of goals*

Chapter 10: Naked Conversations—Harvesting Contention * *Why enduringly successful people seek it out * Contention as an employee perk * Turning your next fight into a feast * Making sure the best idea wins * Don't be right—be effective * It's all about shining eyes*

Chapter 11: Creating Alignment—The Environment Always Wins * *Anything worth doing can't be done alone * Recruiting a team to your dream * Relationships built to last * Why you really are only as good as your people * Don't believe in words—believe in behaviors * In search of the miraculous * Understanding incentives really matters * The final secret*

The Pleasure of Finding Things Out—A Look at the Research Behind *Success Built to Last*

Endnotes

Biographical Index

Index

FOREWORD

Although success can easily be defined as the achievement of goals, there's a difference between temporary and lasting success. I don't think you achieve lasting success unless you add another ingredient to the mixture, and that is to serve a cause greater than yourself. That's what lasting success is all about.

I can't tell you the number of people I have met who have been very successful in the pursuit of wealth, but late in the day began to sense that they didn't really succeed. And yet, I have known people from all degrees of financial wealth who have dedicated themselves to causes greater than themselves and their own self-interests who have led a very satisfying life.

In my book, *Character Is Destiny: Inspiring Stories Every Young Person Should Know and Every Adult Should Remember* (Random House, 2005), we wrote stories about different kinds of qualities that make up a person's character, based on the lives of people that you've probably never heard of—such as Sister Antonio, who resides in a jail in Tijuana taking care of people—to people we all know, such as Mark Twain.

In *Success Built to Last: Creating a Life that Matters*, you will find practical wisdom drawn from the stories of hundreds of the world's most remarkable and enduringly successful people who the authors actually interviewed. This is a book that will make a difference.

Senator John McCain

PREFACE TO THE PAPERBACK EDITION

As we write this, it is not quite a year since the final manuscript for the hardcover edition of *Success Built to Last* was transmitted to Tim Moore at Wharton School Publishing. It has been a year of continuous learning.

We are grateful to Amazon for selecting our book as one of the top three, worldwide, business category, 2007 and for *Business Week* placing it in the top five. The most rewarding feedback is that people are reading the book. Many tell us they wish they had read this book twenty years ago. So do we—we wish we had learned what we have from researching and writing this book twenty years ago! To paraphrase a banking commercial, the trick to life is learning how to be good at the things that matter to you soon enough for it to do you some good!

While it is easy to be critical of today's insatiable appetite for sound bites, there is something to be said for the discipline thus imposed. Talk shows and press interviews require us to hone in on the research findings that carry the most powerful learning for our lives. The always-asked question, "what can our listeners do, starting today, to build lasting success?" has become a question we keep asking ourselves and for which we are learning new answers daily.

Success Built to Last was never intended to be a volume of tips, tools, and techniques. It is a book of ideas drawn from the lives of amazing people. As transaction-focused tips, tools, and techniques become faltering fads, quality ideas last and inform. This year has been filled richly with readers and clients letting us know the ways in which the ideas presented throughout the book have been put to work in their lives, organizations, and communities. We have seen a convergence of ideas developed into practices that make an immediate difference.

For example, the ideas that "it's dangerous not to do what you love" and "whatever you are be a good one," combined with a commitment to a deliberate practice, become a transformative process for building a wonderful life and effective organizations. We define a deliberate practice as doing what you love to do with the intention of becoming good at it. This is the essence of achieving mastery in any field.

Contrary to conventional wisdom about the nature of talent, emerging research suggests that you do not possess a natural gift for a certain job, because targeted natural gifts don't exist. British-based researchers Michael J. Howe, Jane W. Davidson, and John A. Sluboda conclude in an extensive study, "The evidence we have surveyed . . . does not support the [notion that] excelling is a consequence of possessing innate gifts." By embracing a thoughtfully designed, deliberate practice, you can make yourself into any number of possibilities—you can even make yourself great. Once you are clear on what you are deeply passionate about, talent has little or nothing to do with greatness. On the other hand, work has everything to do with it. In this very real sense, talent is built and not born.

In *Built to Last* Collins and Porras described the women and men who created visionary companies as *Builders*—they continuously developed the capabilities of their people and organizations. This is certainly true of the men and women in *Success Built to Last*. The reality that talent is built and not born demands that the learning and development processes in organizations be reinvented to more effectively facilitate building talent. This is an opportunity for human resource professionals to make the kind of contribution to the organizations and people whom they serve and that we know they hunger to make.

Ongoing research by gifted scientists is constantly upgrading our knowledge about how the human mind-brain-body complex functions interdependently, along with how to develop practices that enable the application of this understanding to build richer lives and societies. We are learning, for example, how the way in which we use our mind actually causes physical changes in our brain. That is to say, as we develop a disciplined mind, our brain physically grows larger in the areas that process the content of our focused attention. Think of this as bodybuilding for the brain. The result is an enhanced ability to discern and create what our mind invests meaning in. It is quite literally true that as you train your mind, you physically change your brain in important ways that powerfully shape your future.

This means we really do have an extraordinary potential to transform ourselves, our organizations, and our societies. We offer *Radical Mentoring* and one-on-one coaching programs built around this research. You will find more information about this and other programs that enable the process of building high-performance teams and organizations at www.successbuilttolast.com. The site is regularly updated to incorporate ongoing research and breakthrough applications.

This book is also a book about leadership, a topic on which so much has been written that it has become difficult to integrate a diverse collection of viewpoints into a set of practices that are immediately useful in the rigorous demands of daily living and business life. In the context of *Success Built to Last* we regard all the people in this book as leaders and their stories chronicle journeys of leadership. Clearly all of these extraordinary men and women place at the leading edge of the bell curve of achievement.

To put it another way, all of them live at the leading edge of what we would call high performance—although "performance" has become an overused word that fails to precisely describe the way that these people live and work in the world. Even making the separation "life and work" is artificial because these people live a seamless life—they do not divide and compartmentalize the various dimensions of their lives into categories such as career, family, friends, etc. They bring themselves as whole people to every aspect of their lives. We counsel the executives we coach to bring all of themselves to the office and every part of their lives. Enduring success demands this of us all.

Another way to think about this is that these very accomplished people excel at the art of alignment in their lives. They are clear about what matters to them, what they are deeply passionate about, and what they choose to invest meaning in. This idea of meaning being a personal resource to be deliberately invested is huge. Too often we seek external decrees that cover what is supposed to matter to us and what has meaning. Consequently we take on a life that is not our own at which we can never succeed. The people with whom we had conversations that formed the basis of our exploratory research for *Success Built to Last* don't think or act this way. They define success in very personal terms and invest meaning as a sacred resource. They possess very different *ThoughtStyles* and *ActionStyles* from those belonging to people who have not yet created a wonderful life for themselves.

Moreover when faced with alternative paths of action, the people of *Success Built to Last* choose in favor of what matters to them—they act with integrity to meaning. This process of aligning *Meaning*, *Thought*, and *Action* to achieve three overlapping and largely concentric circles is their continuous practice. It is at the heart of success built to last.

We have come to think about this book as a living document rather than a finished volume. Yes, the book itself is printed, bound, and in this sense "final." On the other hand the Internet enables updates, resources—and dare we say it—tips and tools to be made continuously available.

Visit us at www.successbuilttolast.com and you will receive valuable free content. You will also find video clips that bring further to life the ideas in this book. Join with us in growing a community of people sharing their stories as they build successful lives and gain an opportunity to contribute to others by sharing your own story if you wish to.

The world really does need you to be successful in creating a life that matters. We invite you to use this book and our companion Web site as your personal resource for enduring success.

Jerry Porras
Stewart Emery
Mark Thompson

June 1st, 2007

ACKNOWLEDGEMENTS

As we visited with remarkable people all over the world, we were struck over and over again by the notion that no one does anything that matters alone. This book is no exception. We're grateful for all the talented people who made this journey possible for us. They have all been great partners and many have become good friends. Wharton School Publishing Publisher Tim Moore brought us the resources of the world's largest publisher, Pearson Education, and generously provided valuable coaching and advice.

Equally important, he made a great team available for *Success Built to Last*. We give special thanks to Amy Neidlinger (marketing manager), Gina Kanouse (managing editor), Christy Hackerd (project editor), Sarah Kearns (copy editor), Sheri Cain (proofreader), Lisa Stumpf (indexer), Gloria Schurick (senior compositor), Chuti Prasertsith (cover designer), Dan Uhrig (manufacturing buyer), and Susie Abraham (editorial assistant). Russ Hall (development editor) helped us make our intentions in the text crisper, sharper, and livelier, and we look forward to collaborating on many more adventures.

We are grateful to Jim Collins, coauthor of *Built to Last*, whose continuing passion to contribute to leadership and management development, through learning and teaching, further inspired and informed this work.

Thanks also to Dean Robert Joss and the Graduate School of Business at Stanford University—the epicenter of our efforts—along with Professor Cliff Nass of the Stanford School of Humanities, for their encouragement to create an interdisciplinary book project that spans the business and the social sciences worlds.

Professor Jerry Wind at The Wharton School gave us expert guidance and fresh perspective on our secondary research. This made it possible to conduct a *World Success Survey* with a world-class team under the leadership of the Dr. Howard Moskowitz, whose research at Harvard evolved into a career as one of the leading scientists in his field. The i-Novation division of Moskowitz Jacobs included an amazingly talented crew of researchers, including Barbara Itty, Rachel Katz, Chris Pomponi, and Alex Gofman. As we turned the survey into prose, Moskowitz added the technical writing skills and ideas of Charles Loesch, director of Marketing Research at FiSite Research.

We are indebted to Chuck Schwab for making it possible for Mark Thompson to create the Schwab CEO Series and to engage in the World Economic Forum and the Republican and Democratic national conventions. These events made this project inevitable and the subject of success even more irresistible.

We are grateful for the talents of Richard Wilson, who produced many of these interviews with Mark and who, along with leadership expert Terry Pearce, inspired him to expand this adventure to engage with remarkable people from so many different fields, faiths, and walks of life.

Bonita Thompson, our research director, poured through hundreds of hours of digital recordings and hundreds of pages of transcripts. Her passionate and tireless data analysis yielded ideas as diverse as *the cause has charisma* and the identification of the three circles, *Meaning*, *Thought*, and *Action*. Her diverse background—embracing behavioral psychology, human resources, information systems, statistical analysis, and business—contributed rich context and methodology to the book's structure.

Joan Emery provided us with feedback about what made a difference (and what didn't) in this manuscript based on her great community network, along with her decades of coaching individuals and teams to find their greater potential in nonprofit and corporate settings. Joan also discovered that the ideas and practices set forth in this book not only serve critical issues that impact careers and organizations, but also families and teenagers for whom this work has become a valuable resource.

We want to thank Frank Patitucci for introducing Stewart Emery to Jerry Porras, and Denise Thomas for introducing Stewart to Mark Thompson. Without these serendipitous events, this book would not have been written. Thank you to Professor Klaus Schwab, Frances Hesselbein, Marshall Goldsmith, Jack Canfield, Dave Pottruck, Davia Nelson, Baylee DeCastro, Jason Jennings, Senator John McCain, President Jimmy Carter, Visa's Susanne Lyons, and the New York Stock Exchange's Carie Crandall for so many important introductions and illuminating questions that informed our inquiry.

We feel blessed and grateful to have so many remarkable people participate in these interviews over the past decade, from those who toil out of the limelight in communities of need, such as Norma Hotaling and Brother David Steindl-Rast, to those who are household names on very different journeys, such as Richard Branson, Steve Forbes, Maya Angelou, Herb Kelleher, Nelson Mandela, and The Dalai Lama. (A summary of participants can be found in the biographical index at the end of this book, and more information is available at www.SuccessBuiltToLast.com.)

We want to thank everyone we have had the privilege to meet and know in creating this work. We have been forever changed by your insights. We have only just begun.

With gratitude,
Jerry Porras, Stewart Emery, and Mark Thompson
Stanford, California
June, 2006

SUCCESS BUILT TO LAST

INTRODUCTION

From *Built to Last* to *Success Built to Last*

The Mandela Effect

It was close to midnight at the World Economic Forum when we sat down to wait for the last meeting of the day. The freezing rain had turned to a blizzard, but inside it felt like noon in the Sahara as the heating system gushed to overcompensate. Mark Thompson was nodding off in his chair when Nelson Mandela suddenly appeared around the corner, extending a sweaty hand and a tired smile. Thompson shivered as Mandela leaned on his shoulder and eased onto the leather couch.

In the years before Mandela, an activist lawyer, had been sent to a death camp, he was rarely without zealous overconfidence about his mission to end apartheid. South Africa had suffered violence and unrest that seemed irreconcilable. Although Mandela initially advocated a peaceful solution, he eventually took up arms when the path of peace appeared to be a dead end. In 1964, he was convicted of conspiracy and sabotage and sentenced to life imprisonment.

Most of his years as an inmate were on Robben Island, off Cape Town, where the South African government sent the opposition to break its morale. During his many years of hard labor, the government pressed him repeatedly to compromise his beliefs in exchange for early freedom. He refused.

After 27 years in captivity, in 1990, at the age of 71, Mandela was released. He had every reason to have become the most dangerous man on his continent, but instead he accelerated the peaceful reinvention of his nation.

How could he have overcome his hatred to lead a non-violent revolution, seeking reconciliation instead of revenge? There he sat, exhausted, but radiant; continuing his quest to heal his homeland. The adulation of Mandela's fans has grown or evaporated, depending on whom you ask. Nevertheless, he took his own unique path—a journey that matters so much to him that he has stayed the course year after year, often despite the social and political conse-quences, not because of them. When he could be lounging in retirement, the Nobel Laureate and ex-President was instead recruiting people to his cause—as he had been doing not just for a month or a year, but for a lifetime, with an intensity that had not faded despite his decades of suf-fering in a South African jail.

Your three co-authors, separately and now together, have always been passionately curious about what makes enduringly successful people and extraordinary organiza-tions tick. We have long shared a common question: What inspires long-term achievers to make the kind of choice Mandela did—to struggle and grow despite all odds—to find new meaning and hang onto it not just for the moment or for himself, but to create success that lasts? Although history supports Mandela's noble intentions, the fact that he didn't start out as a saint, with neither perfect grace, nor humility, before his long walk to freedom, makes his jour-ney even more useful and inspiring to the rest of us. That's the *Mandela Effect*—when you can create enduring success not because you are perfect or lucky but because you have the courage to do what matters to you.

From Built to Last *to* Success Built to Last

Mandela's transformation is a courageous example of creating a life built to last. He achieved not just any success, but enduring success that lasts because it matters. In the introduction for the paperback edition of the business classic, *Built to Last,* Jim Collins and Jerry Porras reported "a significant number of people had found key concepts useful in their personal and family lives as they approached the fundamental human issues of self-identity and self-renewal. Who am I? What do I stand for? What is my purpose? How do I maintain my sense of self in this chaotic, unpredictable world? How do I infuse meaning into my life and work? How do I remain renewed, engaged, and stimulated?"[1]

Healthy, sustainable societies require the creation of healthy, sustainable organizations, and great organizations and societies can only be built by human beings who can grow and create meaningful success. If you believe that—and we do—then talking to people who had remarkable lives and lasting impact seemed a natural thing to do. As inner-city educator Marva Collins (no relation to Jim) told us, when you create a life that matters—a life you feel worthy of living—then "the world would be a darker place without you."

And so began the journey of our collaboration on *Success Built to Last.*

> *Healthy, sustainable societies require the creation of healthy, sustainable organizations, and great organizations and societies can only be built by human beings who can grow and create meaningful success.*

Conversations with Enduringly Successful People

This book is based on interviews with over 200 people all over the world who have made a difference—large or small—in their field, profession, or community, but who have lived a life that they believe mattered. In these conversations, we rediscovered a principle that is starting to emerge in books about organizational performance and leadership, but rarely seems fully developed: Success in the long run has less to do with finding the best idea, organizational structure, or business model for an enterprise, than with discovering what matters to us as individuals. It is here, at a very personal level, where thought and feeling inform each other, that creativity begins, and where the potential for enduring organizations emerges. We found ourselves on a quest to find insights —probing to uncover the principles and practices of individuals whose impact on the world endures.

These people are not confined to the categories of entrepreneur, revolutionary, or positive deviant. Many are reluctant to think of themselves as leaders or role models even today. Most did not start out by pursuing success as conventionally defined by their culture. Some will probably never have much money; others are rich, even very rich, but very few started out wealthy. They come from many backgrounds, some horrific and others privileged.

In terms of personality, they're all over the map—some are naturally loud and assertive, while others are barely audible until you ask them about what matters to them. A few have so-called charisma, but most do not; and many remain introverts in the midst of success. At some point in their lives, all of them found themselves on a collision course with a kind of need that generated a relentless, passionate conviction to change the way things are for the long run, often despite how society might judge them.

We struggled with how to refer to these enduring high achievers. Labels such as "visionary leader," in this context, seemed unnecessarily lofty; creating a separation that would provide the rest of us with reasons not to reach inside ourselves to retrieve our greater possibilities. Let's be clear, however, that all of these people are providing leadership in one way or another. Ultimately, we chose the terms "Enduringly Successful People" and "Builders," the latter a description based in part on the "clock-builder" concept from the original *Built to Last* book. By way of metaphor, Collins and Porras made a distinction between the ability to tell the time in the moment and the ability to build a clock that could tell the time beyond the lifetime of the builder. They observed that leaders who created a vision and culture that endured were "clock-builders" whose organizations stood the test of time, outlasted them as individuals, and ultimately outperformed those organizations run by men and women who functioned merely as "time tellers" who lead in the traditional manner hoping to succeed with a hot idea.

Builders are people whose beginnings may be inauspicious but who eventually become defined by their creativity. At some point in their lives, Builders feel compelled to create something new or better that will endure throughout their lifetime and flourish well beyond. Builders often see themselves simply as people trying to make a difference doing something that they believe deserves to be done with or without them, and they recruit the team—build the organization—needed to get it done. Great organizations can be a dividend of this process, but enduring institutions seem to be more of an outcome of the Builder's mindset than a goal in and of itself.

We learned that, for the most part, extraordinary people, teams, and organizations are simply ordinary people doing extraordinary things that matter to them. The message here is that you have it within you to live an

> *We learned that, for the most part, extraordinary people, teams, and organizations are simply ordinary people doing extraordinary things that matter to them.*

extraordinary life. You have the choice to embrace a personally meaningful journey, integrating your personal and professional lives in ways that make a lasting difference. And when you do that, you have the potential to create an organization and a legacy that can serve the world long after you're gone.

How We Found the People

We interviewed relatively unknown business managers, entrepreneurs, teachers, Olympians, and Nobel Laureates, as well as Pulitzer, Grammy, Peabody, and Academy Award winners and the CEOs of large and small organizations. We met many of these people during consulting assignments around the world. To identify additional people to interview, we reviewed an eclectic variety of well-established lists—from *Time Magazine*'s *Most Influential People* to Oprah Winfrey's *Use Your Life Award* winners, as well as those on the annual honor rolls of the biggest, fastest growing, or most admired in major business publications, notably *Forbes* and *Fortune*. We also looked at lists of noteworthy individuals honored by nonprofit organizations.

From this universe of people, we overlaid an unusual time limitation to our review—a 20-year minimum—eliminating those who had significant success in their careers, with a few exceptions, for less than two decades. As a result, we dropped celebrities-of-the-moment and multiple generations of charismatic leaders who come and go—culling our list to fewer than a thousand people who described themselves as having found lasting success.

From that group, we screened for diversity of interests, industries, and gender. We invited several hundred people to participate and, ultimately, completed more than 200 personal interviews from 1996 to 2006.[2] Not surprisingly, the group was largely over age 40, and the oldest individual interviewed was 95.

Avoiding the Apprentice Trap

In the age of reality TV, it has become commonplace for individuals to rise from complete obscurity to superstardom in a matter of weeks or months, only to soon disappear into the "where are they now?" files—or worse. We looked at people with a long tenure of performance—people who mattered year after year—rather than anyone who happened to show up on the cover of this week's magazine as a celebrity-of-the-moment from *The Apprentice* or *Survivor.*

This long-term approach allowed us to include people who have had significant impact, both those who are popular as well as those who are wildly out of fashion, but nonetheless well worth interviewing for this project because they have (or had) been highly accomplished in their field for a long time. Jimmy Carter was stunned by a humiliating defeat—a landslide against him in the 1980 elections—but found a more rewarding role and won the Nobel Peace Prize after 20 more years of following an entirely new dream largely unrelated to his presidency. Although he's under fire again for his strongly held views and his latest book on values and anti-fundamentalism, he continues his mission around the world.

There are bound to be people who you may think are inappropriate choices for this discussion about enduring success. Whether you love them or hate them, very few of the people we interviewed will escape harsh criticism from one quarter or another because they are, by definition, having impact doing what matters to them! Indeed, as soon as you place someone on a pedestal as a role model, there seems to be a perverse law of the universe that increases the chances that person or that organization will stumble foolishly or become the target of heated controversy. Let's make it clear that the people interviewed are not presented here as role models for you to follow. That's a very personal choice only you can make. We offer them only to provoke a discussion that you may need to have with yourself, and the people who matter to you, about the definition of success. If there is anything that became abundantly clear after so many interviews, it was that there are many different, even contradictory and dangerous, ways to go about evaluating success that lasts—as you will see in Chapter 1, "From Great to *Lasting*—Redefining Success."

Many high achievers who have enduring success cherish a dogma with which we disagree, and some that were even offensive to us. We hope you can't tell who they are. We excluded violent criminals and terrorists who have had impact for the long haul because we hope that none of us can or should count on insanity or other criminal pathologies to build a legacy of lasting impact.

Successful People Have a History of Mistakes and They Harvest Their Failures

What often surprises most people is that Builders have very significant failures, losses, and bitter disappointments. Some are experiencing difficulty as we publish this book. In hundreds of interviews, we never met a soul who didn't have embarrassments or failures in their portfolio of experience, including the authors themselves. Extraordinary individuals take one step back and two steps forward with most every challenge—and sometimes two steps back to one step forward. They harvest useful lessons and knowledge from what doesn't work, and they display a remarkable resiliency; an ability to bounce back from adversity.

They don't just think positively, but rather practice the ability to respond and move ahead, often despite how they might feel in the moment, whether the setback was their own foolish fault or just an unlucky break. Builders generally did not blame others for their circumstances, but instead focused their attention on actions within their control that they could take to solve or manage the problem.

This sense of perspective was particularly necessary during our first set of interviews. As you might expect, a few of these high achievers seemed superhuman. They were not remotely like the vast majority of the rest of us on Earth. Some people are way too smart, talented, or lucky to be helpful as a reference. An unnerving number of Nobel Laureates and virtuosos came into this world with their special genius seemingly in full bloom. If you yearn for the heights of Yo Yo Ma, you had better be a cello prodigy by age seven. "No novelist in the world would have dared invent him. The combination of virtues—musical, intellectual, and personal is simply too implausible," said *Smithsonian Magazine*.[3] He is a generous humanitarian who lives his values and is an incredibly disarming and warm person when you meet him. These are gifts, but the rest of his talents are simply out of the reach for almost all of us, and, therefore, not as useful a source as others might be.

We certainly didn't want to take this journey just to find more people who give further reason to doubt our own abilities and reason to remain anonymous. Fortunately, and to our great relief, in the process of meeting and interviewing hundreds of remarkably successful people, we uncovered good news. We found powerful principles that transcend luck or simply great genes. In Chapter 1, we share a simple, three-part theoretical framework that explores useful attributes that all these successful people have in common.

Tracking these people down wasn't easy. Some work in remote regions of the world and surface only occasionally; others are celebrities or leaders whose schedules are in high demand. We intercepted some during their visits to universities around the world. Many we met initially during business conferences and consulting assignments. We interviewed people in the field, at conferences, public radio stations, or in their homes, offices, limos, and studios in the United States, Asia, and Europe.

Throughout this book, you will see descriptions of the places and circumstances in which we interviewed people. We have provided that additional color because we believe that, whenever possible, it's important to observe the ways these individuals actually behave—not just what they say. We wanted to catch them in the act of doing (or not doing) what they said they do—for example, Mandela's willingness to entertain a bunch of caffeinated business suits and other leaders at the World Economic Forum to continue to fuel the global dialog about peace and freedom.

For many years, we have participated in the Forum, which is a four-day marathon in the January snow three hours from Zurich, where attendees run from early morning espresso to well past midnight, often standing in lines oddly packed with CEOs, social workers, billionaires, and Nobel Laureates—awaiting access to venues—all anxious to squeeze in quality time with rock stars, heads of state, and each other. This sounds like a spectacle, and sometimes it is, but it's one of the more effective places to connect with people who are having lasting impact. What keeps you going despite the high security and long hours is the intellectual feast—dining all day and night on the insights and eccentricities of some of the world's most enduringly successful people.

Our Approach to the Interviews

After we found Builders to interview, we needed a fresh way to think about this topic. We did not want to rely entirely on third-party biographies or send out yet another survey with a request to tick boxes on a mass mailing. We're not sure those surveys get the full attention of the leaders they're sent to anymore and, as Peter Drucker warned us, "That's all been done before." Drucker (and many others) encouraged us to think differently about this—to pursue free-ranging conversations with a diverse group of people about what success means rather than focus on business leaders or leadership per se. Until you "figure out what success means" to you personally and to your organization, leadership is an almost "pointless conversation," Drucker admonished. And we definitely did not want to confirm our own set of beliefs about some theory we were trying to prove. We wanted to learn!

> Until you "figure out what success means" to you personally and to your organization, leadership is an almost "pointless conversation," Drucker admonished.

The fact that we actually interviewed the vast majority of our sources, rather than rely on surveys or third-party data, sets this work apart from other offerings in this field. We explored the issues personally with individuals as human beings, asking them one kick-off question about their definition of success and lasting leadership. This open-ended inquiry enabled each enduringly successful person, or Builder, rather than the authors, to drive the conversation and provide insights in ways that would have never occurred otherwise. We followed their lead by asking clarifying questions to reveal the depth and creativity of their answers, rather than sticking to our own preset agenda of questions. All too often in academic research, dialog is curtailed when a respondent moves beyond the preordained questions or topic. We wanted to mine the richness of that spontaneous dialog.

The unique power of this project was that it did not start out as a science experiment, but was the culmination of many leadership interviews collected in the course of our intensive, face-to-face consulting work in a wide variety of organizations, at universities, at professional conferences, for public broadcasting programs, and at other eclectic settings over a ten-year period. We saw the resulting data set as a gold mine of information that, when systematically analyzed, yielded some incredible insights. This opportunistic approach provided a very different and, we believe, richer dialog than if we had started with a narrower, highly structured process. The conversations exposed us to viewpoints that we never would have thought of as theories to test. In a real sense, this journalistic approach gave us a better set of hypotheses and a fresh perspective on the issues of leadership and lasting success.

By approaching people with this kind of exploratory dialog, we learned more than we could have hoped for or imagined. In fact, we found it sometimes unsettling, and occasionally threatening, to hear highly accomplished people describe things we had believed to be universal and concrete—like core values and the definition of success—in many different and even contradictory ways. The values these people cling to are their own intuitive and artful interpretation of what matters to them. The beliefs that they defended so dearly were not facts of life, but daring choices—judgments about what was right for them, not what everyone else should do. As we listened to their stories, we felt the bondage of our own beliefs dissolve.

After completing the interviews, we analyzed the content in a structured way to find the most frequent patterns of behavior and thinking, identifying 21 broad topic categories[4] that emerged from the conversations. The strongest of these made it into this book.

In *Success Built to Last,* we could not follow in the footsteps of many business books in which companies are paired for comparison and measured in terms of relative performance based on their business model, growth rates, founding data, key competitors, operating efficiency, or stock market or other relative financial data. In our interviews, we reached out to individuals who work not just for public companies listed on stock exchanges, but also private for-profit and nonprofit organizations, scientific and educational institutions, government agencies, and communities. As a practical matter, we didn't think it was reasonable to have a control group to compare human beings in those same ways—as winners, losers, or runners-up.

Instead, with our manuscript already drafted, we tested our assumptions by creating a unique independent survey to challenge our conclusions. To take this ambitious step, our Stanford-based team partnered with Prentice Hall/Pearson Education, Wharton School Publishing (WSP), Lauder Professor Yoram (Jerry) Wind, editor of WSP and director of the SEI Center for Advanced Studies in Management at the Wharton School, and survey expert Dr. Howard Moskowitz and a team of researchers at the Moskowitz Jacobs design lab. Moskowitz's groundbreaking research at Harvard led him to author 14 books and 300 papers based in part on a sophisticated survey technique called conjoint analysis and rule developing experimentation (RDE). It's been around since the 1970s, but Moskowitz has been using this technique to reduce the tendency for people who answer surveys to give politically correct responses—digging instead into the soft underbelly of beliefs rather than what people think is appropriate or polite to say. His design lab uses it on everything from consumer products to presidential elections and views about terrorism.

Our *World Success Survey* was made available online on April 18, 2006, to executives and educators at senior and junior levels who are Knowledge@Wharton subscribers.

More than 365 people from around the globe responded within the first week. This independent sample of data provided a comparison set and validation for our interview findings, and showed significant differences in perceptions and mindsets between respondents categorized as "successful" or "unsuccessful" in their professional or personal lives.

Among the top line results were confirmation that successful people don't rely on the approval of others to pursue their cause or calling. They have the audacity to take the initiative despite social pressures rather than because of them. They are more emotionally committed to doing what they love than being loved by others. They don't wallow or obsess on a single defeat or rely on finding scapegoats or blame when things go wrong, but instead relentlessly place highest priority on being effective in getting the outcomes they are seeking. (As we discuss in Chapter 7, "The *Tripping* Point—Always Make New Mistakes," and Chapter 8, "Wounds to Wisdom—Trusting Your Weaknesses and Using Your Core Incompetencies," Builders "harvest" their failures and successes as data they can use to improve their effectiveness.) Successful people also said that "loving what you do" is a necessary condition for success. (Indeed, in Chapter 2, "Love It or Lose—Passions and the Quest for Meaning," we review the dangers of not doing what you love because people who have that passion can outlast and eventually outrun you in the task.)

Regardless of whether the survey participants rated themselves as "successful" or "unsuccessful," all groups said that the traditional dictionary definition of success—notably wealth, fame, and power—no longer describes what success means to them. Although popularity and affluence, for example, are nice outcomes, people prefer to define *success* as the ability to "make a difference," "create lasting impact," and being "engaged in a life of personal fulfillment," according to the study. What is special about Builders is that they won't settle for less than that! (See "The Pleasure of Finding Things Out—A Look at the Research Behind *Success Built to Last*.")

Perhaps most important, it is our hope that this book and the *World Success Survey* launch an international dialog—providing a forum for this important subject that empowers people to be heard with their own voices for the first time, together, on every continent. This extra step—to reach out to engage with the rest of the world in a conversation about redefining success—continues to keep us mindful, particularly when we find ourselves leaping to conclusions in a vacuum. *Science* in the social sciences can never escape influence from the personal realities of the people doing the work. Authors on leadership would love to convince you that they've been able to create the ultimate recipe for the secret sauce of success, but no one can give you that.

Why Take This Journey?

We made a conscious decision to find and share insights without being prescriptive for a change. This is like a dinner conversation. Our intent here is to provoke a deeper dialog about success and what matters in our lives, rather than yet another lecture about leadership pretending to offer all the answers.

What we can tell you is we have been deeply touched and forever changed by the spirit, principles, and practices of the people we've met. We invite you to enter into the world of what follows unburdened by the need to believe or disbelieve. Rather, allow yourself to be inspired to find your own way. We hope you can challenge conventional wisdom and unearth new possibilities for success that lasts in your life, relationships, and work.

When you opened this book, you may have not intended to discover or be reminded that you are—or have an even bigger opportunity to be—a Builder, just like the enduringly successful people you will read about here. We hope the stories herein will make this clear—leaving you no place to hide—moving you to stretch toward your highest aspirations.

C H A P T E R   1

From Great to *Lasting*—
Redefining Success

"It was another sleepless night followed by another cruel morning. We were running out of money, and I worried constantly about all the people who had sacrificed to come to work for me. They came and they toiled through the night and struggled to make ends meet for their families. The pressure was overwhelming—sometimes, I had to stop and throw up in the gutter on the way to the office."

Keeping his dream going was the hardest thing he had ever tried to do in this life. Ed Penhoet had been comfortable as a biochemist and a professor, then reinvented himself as an entrepreneur and found himself barely keeping a fledgling firm afloat. Things would get worse before they got better, and he seriously considered merging with another equally desperate competitor or giving up entirely.

"Famous executives out there fundamentally gild the lily. They don't tell you the awful truth about the pain you will face. They want you to think they're brilliant and that they had it figured all out at the beginning. That's revisionist history. They might have had a clue, but that's barely all they had." Penhoet was teetering on the edge of a humiliating collapse of everything he had worked 24/7 to achieve. He could lose it all. Success as traditionally defined was not even a concept at this point. What Ed faced was the opposite of success—had he looked up the word "success" in the dictionary, he would have scored zero.

> "Famous executives out there fundamentally gild the lily. They don't tell you the awful truth about the pain you will face."

Why did he persist? It was not just because he was stubborn. There was something bigger than success at stake. When his favorite uncle died from cancer, he had long ago launched a career in biochemistry, determined to find new ways to bring basic research to the marketplace. That was a lifelong cause that had meaning uniquely to him. It was the way Penhoet would create a life that matters.

Creating a life that matters is what most everybody wants. It's the subtitle of this book because it's exactly what we heard from enduringly successful people all over the world. *Builders,*[†] as we call them, do things because they want to build a meaningful life. They want to create a life that matters, and one of the greatest tests of that conviction comes in those dark moments like those that Ed Penhoet suffered in the early days of his start-up. These are the times when Builders don't feel successful—at least not in the traditionally defined terms of popularity, wealth, or influence. Yet they nevertheless choose to remain committed to what they care about despite success, not because of it. When faced with what they discover is so important to them, they summon the courage (or foolishness) to persist because it matters to them.

It's Time to Redefine Success

In fact, we discovered that for most Builders, the culturally accepted measures of success that you find in the dictionary have never been what they were seeking. The standard

---

†   The terms "Builders" and "enduringly successful people" are used interchangeably in this book to describe people who define their own success and have achieved lasting impact in their field for at least 20 years.

description must have been written for budding sociopaths. It is defined as

1. The achievement of something planned or attempted.
2. Impressive achievement, especially the attainment of fame, wealth, or power.
3. Something that turns out as planned or intended.
4. Somebody who has a record of achievement, especially in gaining wealth, fame, or power.[1]

Notice that nowhere in the dictionary definitions do you find any reference to finding meaning, fulfillment, happiness, and lasting relationships. No mention of feeling fully alive while engaged and connected with a calling that matters to you. No thoughts about creating a legacy of service to the world. Yet those are all realities that people who have lasting success say they value most in life and work.

For Builders, the real definition of success is a life and work that brings personal fulfillment and lasting relationships and makes a difference in the world in which they live. The question is why the rest of us tolerate any other definition.

Folks who chase a fantastic but vain hope for fame, wealth, and power—for its own sake—may even achieve it, only to become miserable and pathetic people. Not that there is anything wrong with that, as Seinfeld would say, but we think that the current definition of success is a potentially toxic prescription for your life and work. It is a description that makes you feel more like a failure than a success if it's the standard against which all meaning in your life is measured.

Sure, you might be a little strange if you did not enjoy the "impressive achievement" of something that you "planned or intended." But when you talk with Builders, you will hear that

> *The current definition of success is a potentially toxic prescription for your life and work.*

wealth, fame, and power are not actually goals or accomplishments for most of them. Money and recognition are external factors—they are outcomes of passionately working often on an entirely different objective that is often a personal cause or calling, like Ed Penhoet's drive to find successful treatments for cancer. He chose a way of life that embodied his passions, making a difference to him and the world.

It was not just service or ambition; it was both at the same time. Penhoet's passion was also his service to the world. On his journey from academic life to entrepreneur, and now in his current role running a nonprofit, Penhoet channeled his passion and made it a business that changed the status quo in medical research.

And, yes, in case you're wondering, Penhoet and his colleagues eventually enjoyed many of the traditional measures of success, too, such as becoming wealthy, but these measures weren't his focus. Penhoet's lifelong cause inspired the creation of Chiron, the company he cofounded in 1981 and where he ended up serving as CEO longer than any other person ever had in that industry. Chiron is a $1.9 billion biotech innovator, and today, Penhoet is well into his second career as director of his friend Gordon Moore's $5 billion foundation, where he's supporting the sciences, education, and the environment.

To Achieve Success, First Abandon Popular Delusions

When you feel pressure to pursue the elusive outcomes of traditional success, it's often driven by the burden of making a living, pleasing others, or achieving status. Ironically, it appears that success often will fade, vanish, or become the dungeon of your soul unless it is not your primary objective. Builders like Penhoet tell us that when success just means wealth, fame, and power, it doesn't last and it isn't satisfying. If he had let a culturally promoted definition of success be his guide, he doesn't think he would have ever achieved the success that matters to him.

Instead, people who seek to build long-term success by their own definition—Builders—insist that success may never come without a compelling personal commitment to something you care about and would be willing to do with or without counting on wealth, fame, power, or public acceptance as an outcome.

In reality, most Builders are hailed as leaders in their field usually long after they commit to their calling or to a particular way of living in the world that holds special meaning to them. The mainstream media stories about successful people—along with wishful thinking about instant gratification or a magic pill for success—may make it seem as if they were overnight successes, but it rarely happens that way.

Builders mostly toil with every ounce of their energy and persistence, with heart and soul, for their whole lives. They become lovers of an idea they are passionate about—for years and years—creating something that continually seduces them into obsessing over every detail, losing track of the passage of time. In a real sense, it's something that they'd be willing to do for free, for its own sake. Quincy Jones wouldn't give up music if it wasn't popular, nor would Mandela rest until apartheid was crushed. It's hard to retire from an obsession. Jack Welch is no more likely to stop teaching his brand of business than Maya Angelou is likely to stop writing poetry or teaching. They do it because it matters to them.

After being at it for years, and with the coincidence of whatever "it" is becoming popular, success came for some of them as defined in the dictionary. They may now have success as hailed by the culture, but this is a serendipitous outcome rather than an original goal.

Betrayed by Success and Searching for Meaning

Considering this mismatch between the dictionary definition of success and what you as an individual and your organization might actually care about, it shouldn't be a surprise that you might yearn to "make something of yourself," only to find that you're strangely dissatisfied along the way because what you are working so hard for doesn't really matter to you. Indeed, too many people at some point in their lives set goals and go on to achieve them, often brilliantly, only to find that they are mysteriously disappointed, empty, and unhappy.

Could this be why, despite acquiring material luxuries undreamed of even a few decades ago, there is a rising epidemic of clinical depression and suicide among the wealthiest citizens in America, China, and other rapidly growing economies? The World Health Organization predicts that depression will be the second leading cause of disability by 2020—a prediction that is, well, depressing.

How is it possible to achieve the very definition of success and yet find happiness so fleeting? Builders say it's a simple matter of being cheated by the absence of knowing what really matters to you in your life, not just for today, but for today and for the long term. This is why the people who win the lottery have such a terrible track record of staying happy or sober two years later. It's one of the many reasons why nine out of ten start-up companies fail to sustain themselves for the long term and why it's tough to keep a career on track for decades.

It's why most governments are fraught with needless acrimony and inefficiency, said Vaira Vike-Frieberga, president of Latvia. A former psychology professor at the University of Montreal, she noted that, "All too often, legislators launch their grand plans before making sure there is a shared sense of what success means or whether it matters when we get there."

This also may be a reason why many partnerships, including marriages, don't have happy endings. And it may be why Hollywood celebrity becomes synonymous with short-term relationships and long-term addictions.

You read about these folks all the time in *People Magazine* and the *Wall Street Journal*—the lifestyles of the rich, the famous, and the unbelievably disappointed. These are the people who so many of us aspire to be, and yet even these idols find themselves incomplete, feeling much less excited than when they had nothing but the promise of their imagined future.

You either know a person like this, or you are one.

To avoid this poignant dilemma, be careful what you wish for. When achievement for you or your organization comes without meaning, then it doesn't last. Builders experience a success that does not leave them half full, as can often be the case for those who pursue only material treasures or other short-term measures instead of their own internal definition of lasting fulfillment.

Three Essential Elements of Success Built to Last

In hundreds of interviews, we learned that Builders find lasting success when at least three essential elements come into alignment in their lives and work.

The first essential element is *Meaning*. What you do must matter deeply to you in a way that you as an individual define meaning. It's something that you're so passionate about that you lose all track of time when you do it. It's something that you are willing to recruit other people to, but will do it despite criticism and perhaps even secretly do it for free. In fact, you could not be paid to not do it.

"Success is about building lasting relationships and serving others," said Azim Premji, chairman of Wipro in India. He took the reins of the Bangalore-based firm at age 21 when his father died, then turned it from a fledgling hydrogenated cooking fat producer into an almost $2 billion information technology services company.[2] When it comes to creating lasting success in your life and career, Premji asked, "Don't you think that building a meaningful lasting relationship with yourself about what matters to you is a good place to start?"

We'll look at the many ways that Builders strive to build Meaning in Part I, "Meaning—How Successful People Stay Successful."

The second essential element is *ThoughtStyle*—a highly developed sense of accountability, audacity, passion, and responsible optimism. We call it ThoughtStyle. Steve Jobs told us in an interview back before his famous ad campaign: Enduringly successful people "think different." They have a talent, yes, and perhaps some even have a genius. But they also have a ThoughtStyle that supports their special accomplishments.

As Gerard Kleisterlee put it, "When you can organize your thinking around creating real value, and your thoughts remain focused on what is important to creating that value despite all the incoming distractions, crisis, and complexity crashing down all around you...then you're really lucky because you have a sustainable model" for your work and your life. Kleisterlee is chairman, president, and CEO of Royal Philips Electronics in the Netherlands, with over 160,000 employees in 60 countries and 2005 sales of more than $37 billion.

We will focus on ThoughtStyles of Builders in Part II, "ThoughtStyles—Extreme Makeovers Start in Your Head."

The third element is *ActionStyle*: enduringly successful people find effective ways to take action. This is hardly mind-blowing news, but there is more to ActionStyle than first meets the eye. Many Builders told us about times in their lives when they had a clear sense of meaning, but found it almost impossible to make things happen—to turn meaning and thought into action. Be thoughtful about meaning, but don't let that paralyze you.

When you envision something that is meaningful to you that seems to be ideal or perhaps even perfect, sometimes "it's like a beautiful pastry—too lovely to ruin by eating it," said

Alice Waters, the restaurateur and pioneer in organic cooking who, through an initiative called the *Edible Schoolyard*,[3] is determined to change the world one mouthful at a time.

Anyone who has "a perfect picture in his or her head of what must be done and what matters" also knows that the results of acting on that idea might "never be as perfect as that image in their mind," Waters said. The reason this happens is because moving from thought to action puts idealism and beauty at risk as "your dream might lose something in the translation!"

Ultimately, "it's about the pleasure of work itself—we've almost completely forgotten about that. The quality of loving the work is one of the most important values that we can bring to people," Waters said with an appreciative eye on the talented chefs who were passionately tossing, chopping, and stirring lunch in her award-winning restaurant, *Chez Pannise*. They looked like sculptors as they arranged individual masterpieces on each plate.

"Do it because it's worth doing even if you can't quite make it as perfect as your original fantasy," said Jack Jia, who grew up "with nothing but a head full of dreams" in Chengdu in China's Sichuan Province. Today, he's a serial entrepreneur, president of the Hua Yuan Science and Technology Association, and founder and CEO of Baynote. "If you refuse to do something you believe in, your mind will never leave you alone. It just will torment you. If it really matters, you might as well get on with it despite the problems that will occur when you take on a new challenge. Any new beginning, anything creative, will get messy in parts," he said. "If you do it with your eyes wide open, with discipline, it will only get better when you do it more."

That's the way it is, Builders told us countless times. "So, get moving and get on with what you really care about doing."

Without discipline, some overly ambitious folks encounter the opposite problem—all action and no meaning—

cautioned Singapore-based entrepreneur and government advisor, Peng Ong. People who find action irresistible for its own sake often discover they're taking the wrong hill. "You've got to get yourself and your team all on the same page about what success will require of you. Think about what matters and the people you are serving first. Then, organize your thoughts and creativity around that to make it happen." Taking action without stopping first to determine what you hold meaningful is a big reason things don't last. Builders use a special goal-setting process and even encourage contention to help them achieve those aspirations.

We'll focus on these and other *ActionStyles* in Part III, "ActionStyles—Turning Passion Into Action."

Three Simple, But Not Easy, Pieces that Must Fit Together

In our journey toward *Success Built to Last*, we discovered that these three elements—an individually defined Meaning, a creative ThoughtStyle, and an effective ActionStyle— when you have them in alignment, form the foundation on which you build and sustain the experience of success. It seems that you might not need all three aligned to achieve short-term ambitions or success as traditionally defined, but the more that you pull them together, the more likely it is that your success (that must be defined for you by you) will keep going decade after decade.

One way to remember these concepts is to think of these elements as the three primary colors of success built to last. When you overlap the primary colors of red, blue, and green,[4] what do you get? A bright, white light. If there is a "right" target to go after, this is it. Builders don't seek goals for their own sake; they find something that holds great *meaning* for them first, so meaning is on top, informing the rest of the model. Builders manage their *thoughts* in ways that keep them on track and then take relentless *action* in pursuit of what matters to them (meaning). The great opportunity in life and work is to make that target in the center as big as possible by bringing all three circles together and increasing the degree of overlap.

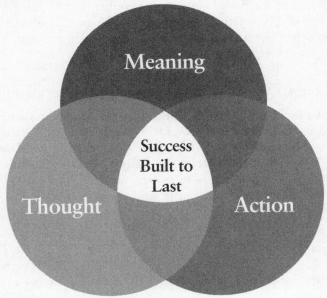

Primary colors of success built to last

Become consciously aware of what matters to you and then rally your *thought* and *action* to support your definition of *meaning*. That is what we call alignment. As these elements come together to constitute a single target of white light, it gets easier to hit the mark in your life and actually experience success that lasts.

Become consciously aware of what matters to you and then rally your thought *and* action *to support your definition of* meaning. *That is what we call alignment.*

Of course, this is a simple model for a very complex and often challenging process. The greater tendency is for these three circles to drift apart wildly out of sync. Without continuous effort, many forces at work and at home make it difficult to keep the alignment together. In the immortal words of Peter Drucker, "The only things that evolve by themselves (in an organization) are disorder, friction, and malperformance."[5]

Teen Detective Meets Ravishing Reporter

When Jane Bryant Quinn, the money columnist and author of *Smart and Simple Financial Strategies for Busy People*, was growing up, she dreamed of becoming Nancy Drew, the heroic teen detective in the Carolyn Keene novels. This beloved character had been solving mysteries since the time when women weren't allowed to do that for a living.

But when Quinn ran across comic strip sleuth Brenda Starr, she traded up on her fantasy. As the glamorous journalist for a daily newspaper, unapologetically called *The Flash*, "Brenda travels the world solving mysteries, unearthing scoops, and stealing the heart of almost every man she meets."[6] Brenda was a career woman before the phrase was even acceptable, let alone fashionable—a smart, competitive, ravishing redhead created by Dale (Dahlia) Messick in 1940 when it wasn't likely for a woman to get a job like that.

"Sounded like the best job in town when I was a teenager," Quinn told us, "A life of adventure, boys, and making a difference all at once." So, when she graduated with a liberal arts degree, she showed up at the doorstep of *Newsweek*.

"It was still legal at that time not to allow a woman to be a reporter," she said. Undaunted, Quinn worked at the mail desk. Her ambition was to work in journalism. That's what mattered to her—to have an extraordinary life and bring the truth to people. "I would live into my dream" even if the world wasn't ready for it yet, she winked.

Quinn made herself more than useful, working behind the scenes on so many stories that she became indispensable to the reporting staff. Eventually, she took advantage of her growing interests in business and finance with a sort of Brenda Starr sense of righteousness about uncovering the dirt, dangers, and rewards of investing—a mission that makes her eyes shine with passion (and sometimes flash with rage) as much today as it did decades ago. That's success built to last.

If Quinn had given in to believing that the only thing that had meaning was an egoistic need to be Brenda Starr on her first day at *Newsweek*—and if she thought that was the only way to turn her dream into action—then that would have been a tough target to hit. Such an attitude would have produced a minimal overlap of the three circles and a small bulls-eye. That would have made it terribly easy to miss the mark, become frustrated, and land in another profession. She might have missed her calling.

That's not to say that you should settle for less. Quinn would argue that she didn't settle at all. That's the point. The toughest thing is to get out of your own way, even if life is incredibly unfair. Things seem to work out better for remarkable people when meaning, thought, and action overlap to create an abundant target for their dreams. Quinn realized that Brenda Starr wasn't a destination; it was a way of life. She went for a bigger long-term prize. Quinn's dedication to Starr's sense of purpose rather than a job title got her on the playing field early, where she could build her skills and demonstrate her talent and creativity.

It didn't bring her popularity in the beginning. A woman advising you about your money didn't get much support 30 years ago. But Jane Bryant Quinn's discipline to trust her head and her heart—to stay wide awake and bring them

> *Most of us worry more about being loved than being what we love.*

into alignment without relying on external adulation—freed her to develop passions that inevitably made her successful by her own definition. She worried less about being loved than being what she loved, and that meant many things to her: a fighter who would unearth injustice, a bestselling author, a wife, and a mother of five. In all parts of her life, Quinn brought together the domains of meaning, thought, and action and, as a result, she went from *great* to *lasting* and helped change the face of financial journalism in America.

Being what we love means doing what matters on and off the job. When Hector de J. Ruiz was busy starting his career and building a life with his wife in the early days, he found himself deeply troubled by the plight of young Hispanics in east Los Angeles. One of the things that greatly mattered to him was the notion that he "always had somebody that was willing to help [him]. That meant a lot to me," he said. "So [at one point], I finally kind of grew up," which to Ruiz meant that he would dedicate himself to helping the disadvantaged go to college despite the personal cost (and even when he had not long ago graduated himself).

"I was making very little money," Ruiz said. But over time, "my wife and I both realized that it seemed like the more of it we did, the easier it got," he said. "A lot of people in east L.A. feel like the Hispanic community is not capable of being able to perform well in some of the things that are required to be effective today in technology. You do a survey of people in east L.A. and they tell you that they are afraid of mathematics. And so I go and talk to these high school kids about the fact that the people who invented the zero were the Maya Indians in Mexico. The people who had one of the most sophisticated architectures in the world were the Aztecs. All of a sudden, you can see these kids beginning to develop a sense of self-worth, and that's what these kids are missing," said Ruiz, who today is CEO of Advanced Micro Devices, with 2005 net sales of $5.8 billion. (He's really good at math, too.) "To be able to in some way contribute to that [before even his own traditionally defined success was assured] has been incredibly rewarding for both my wife and I."

From Great to Lasting

When we first started sharing these principles during the development of *Success Built to Last*, some people feared—and others hoped—we would impose on them celebrity personalities as role models for success, or at the other extreme, we would expect you to become selfless and perfect, whatever that means. That may be a nice aspiration, but this book is not about worshiping the accomplishments of inaccessible, larger-than-life overachievers. That simply doesn't work. Your enduring success is not about following anybody else's roadmap, goals, or achievements. It must be constructed on a foundation of very personal choices that only you can make. None of the people you will meet in the coming pages are being offered as folks you ought to imitate. Take them or leave them, our pledge is to share with you some practices that Builders we met had in common and that work for them. What is more important is that we hope to stimulate a probing dialog about your lasting success and creating a life that matters (to you).

In the process, you may discover you are currently tracking some definition of success never explicitly challenged. It would be a shame for this to remain the unconscious default of your life. Until you compare what really matters to you with what may haunt you about the popular notion of success, your existing concept of both could remain the invisible tyrant you unknowingly resent.

If any of this feels uncomfortable at some point, it could be because of an unexplored gap between what deeply matters to you and what you think the world expects of you. When meaning and success sit together side-by-side out there fully illuminated for your consideration, you suddenly are in a stronger position to demand an answer to the question, "Why am I not doing what matters to me right now?"

It's all too easy to dismiss this line of inquiry. Yet if there was one thing we saw that Builders hold to be true, this would be it: Although many things in life and work are temporary, and nothing seems to last, Builders believe that *meaning* actually does last—forever. They said that what they do (or do not do) while they are here matters. They feel that it might even matter beyond their lifetime.

Let's see what else you have in common with people who have *success built to last*.

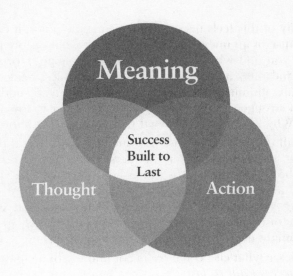

PART I

*Meaning—How Successful People
Stay Successful*

About Meaning and how successful
people stay successful * Passions and the quest for
Meaning * How it's not about balance—it's about
integrity to Meaning * Reconnecting with your
passions to create a life filled with Meaning
(to you)

"Many things in life don't last, but meaning does."

CHAPTER 2

Love It or Lose—Passions
and the
Quest for Meaning

*The only place where you find success before work
is in the dictionary.*
—Mary V. Smith

*Perfection is finally attained not when there is no
longer anything to add, but when there is no longer
anything to take away.*
—Antoine de Saint-Exupery

Much is said today about the importance of loving what you do, but most people simply don't buy it. Sure, it would be nice to do what you love, but as a practical matter, most people don't feel they can afford such a luxury. For many, doing something that really matters to them would be a sentimental fantasy based on wishful thinking.

Listen up—here's some really bad news: It's dangerous not to do what you love. The harsh truth is that if you don't love what you're doing, you'll lose to someone who does! For every person who is half-hearted about their work or relationships, there is someone else who loves what they're half-hearted about. This person will work harder and longer. They will outrun you. Although it might feel

> *Listen up—here's some really bad news: It's dangerous not to do what you love.*

safer to hang onto an old role, you'll find your energy is depleted and, miraculously, you'll be the first in line for the layoffs when they come.

All You Have Is Your Personal Capital

You may have noticed that we now live in a global economy where job security is a contradiction in terms. All you have is your personal capital, and we're not talking about your money. It's your talents, skills, relationships, and enthusiasm. Making success last takes a level of tenacity and passion only love can sustain. Without it, you'll collapse under the weight of the hardship or long-lasting adversity that you are bound to encounter.

Making a life is as important as making a living. This is not an either-or decision. Builders do both. You will hear this from most everyone who has enjoyed lasting success: entrepreneurs, government and religious leaders, artists and educators, single parents, social workers, Academy Award winners, carpenters, store managers, and billionaires.

You will hear it from the most hard-boiled military generals and tough business guys like Larry Bossidy, author of a warm-and-fuzzy-sounding book called *Execution: The Discipline of Getting Things Done*. Bossidy has never been accused of being touchy feely.

On a bitter cold, clear day in Connecticut, we huddled in the tough-minded retired CEO's home office built in a converted barn near a frozen pond, where we talked for hours about success and leadership. When we threw the "L" word at him, the steely eyed former CEO didn't flinch.

"It's a competitive imperative," he insisted. "Only by loving what you do will you actually do more and do it better than the person sitting next to you. If you don't, well then, we'll find someone who does."

Yep, fear is a big motivator, too, but you'll find that love lasts longer. You can run a marathon at gunpoint, but you probably won't win the race.

"You can survive without loving it, but you will be second-rate," said Brigadier General Clara Adams-Ender, Ret. "To spend any part of your career not knowing why you're there will take your power away." It's dangerous not to be fully engaged. If you want to have success that outlasts any job you have, then only love will find the way.

It's Like Saving Up Sex for Old Age

Warren Buffett loved his work long before he had two pennies to rub together. Today, he is one of the richest men on Earth.

"You know, they say that success is getting what you want and happiness is wanting what you get," he said. "Well, I don't know which one applies in this case. But I do know that I wouldn't be doing anything else. I always worry about people who say, 'You know, I'm going to do this for ten years. I really don't like it very well, but I'll do ten more years of this and...' I mean, that's a little like saving up sex for your old age. Not a very good idea," Buffett laughed.

"I tap dance to work and I get down there and I think I'm supposed to lie on my back and paint the ceiling, or something, like Michelangelo, I mean, that's the way I feel. And it doesn't diminish. It's tremendous fun."

The research libraries are filled with studies that confirm that love is not just a warm and fuzzy topic; we're talking about your survival in the competitive marketplace out there, with lots of people who want your job more passionately than you may.

Passionate people spend twice as much time thinking about what they've accomplished, how doable the task ahead is, and how capable they are of it.[1] Your coworkers or competitors who love their work try harder, try more things, move faster, come up with more great ideas,[2] and, frankly, get better opportunities to move up and contribute more than people who only do things for a living.

"The job of leadership today is not just to make money, it's to make meaning," said John Seely Brown, who presided over research for two decades at Xerox Park. "Talented people are looking for organizations that offer not only money, but...spiritual goals that energize...(that) resonate with the personal values of the people who work there, the kind of mission that offers people a chance to do work that makes a difference."

Be warned: The relentless irritation of not loving what you do makes you a pain to be around and has been clinically proven to chip away at your health.

"We spend our health building our wealth," said author and financial advisor Robert T. Kiyosaki, paraphrasing the old proverb. "Then we desperately spend our wealth to hang onto our remaining health." After several successful, but unrelated, entrepreneurial stints, Kiyosaki changed careers again at nearly age 50 to write his first book, *Rich Dad, Poor Dad*, which has sold more than 17 million copies. Wouldn't it be "better to do what we love in the first place so we don't bankrupt our well-being" in a vain attempt to earn our way to freedom?

The Secret of Life

There is a good chance you feel there is something missing in life—or you are on an incessant search for meaning—until you make one simple choice. Those uncertainties can dog you in a never-ending but noble quest until you just go out and serve somebody. Builders from all over the world shared this recurring theme with us.

Frances Hesselbein, chairman and founding president of the Leader to Leader Institute, formerly the Peter F. Drucker Foundation, is best known for her leadership work with large organizations, universities, the U.S. military, and her 13 years as CEO of the Girl Scouts of the United States of America. She led the transformation of that vast nonprofit organization, which today has about 236,000 troops and almost a million volunteers.³ She was awarded the Presidential Medal of Freedom—America's highest civilian honor—in 1998, and was the first recipient of the Dwight D. Eisenhower National Security Series Award in 2002.⁴

Hesselbein, like most Builders, believes that there is "a powerful synergy when you combine service to others with passion for your own mission, your own work."

"We are called to do what we do, and when we respond to that invitation, it is never a job. When we are called to serve and we respond, it is joy and fulfillment," she noted. "The key to fulfillment is service and the key to leadership is not how to do, but rather how to be. Serving others is part of the 'how to be' character of a great leader."

Leadership author Ken Blanchard calls this *Servant Leadership*, wherein the goal of the leader is to promote not herself, but the goals of the organization and careers of the people she leads. It's all about alignment of what's inside your heart and what the world needs. It's about finding what you love and doing that to serve others.

Being in the Zone—The Flow Experience

While researching the book *Flow: The Psychology of Optimal Experience*,⁵ the research team from the University of Chicago, directed by Mihaly Csikszentmihalyi, Ph.D. (a.k.a. Dr. Mike), had a diverse group of people scattered all over the globe wear beepers. The group included farmers, scientists, educators, entrepreneurs, artists, priests, nuns, and government officials. When randomly paged, they were asked to write in a journal what they were doing, together with the quality of their experience at that time.

From a compilation of journal entries gathered from all of the participants, patterns emerged yielding the principles of what was called the *flow experience*. When you are deeply immersed in the process of doing whatever you are doing, and completely lose track of time and place, you are in a flow experience.

> *When you are deeply immersed in the process of doing whatever you are doing, and completely lose track of time and place, you are in a flow experience.*

Athletes describe "being in the zone"—this is also a flow experience. To achieve success built to last, you must cultivate your capacity to be fully alive in your work and, as Jim Kouzes and Barry Posner say in *The Leadership Challenge*, you've got to celebrate your values and passions.

Builders Are More Like Nerds Than Supermodels

With the exception of a few people who are in the business of looking elegant, Builders are more like nerds than supermodels. When you find you've forgotten social graces while doing what you love, then that is probably a clue about your calling in life, or at least you have found one of your passions. Passion is, by its nature, unbalanced and can be unappealing and irritating to people who don't care about your particular passion. If you're a rock star, the life of the world's great research scientists will not appeal to you!

The point is that you know that you are on the right track when you naturally obsess over what you love like a *geek*, as in being a person who is single-minded in a pursuit, at the risk of being socially insensitive while so engaged. It attracts you even when you're too tired to do anything else. It seduces you to the point where you lose interest in everything else, to an extent that you become socially inept around the people who couldn't care less about whatever it is.

Finding and doing the thing you love offers you a very different experience of work. In fact, it may not feel like work at all. Builders typically refer to their work as "tremendous fun." This is a totally different experience than you will have if you're doing what you're doing just because you think you should.

Death by PowerPoint

Places like Stanford University in California's Silicon Valley are crawling with entrepreneurial ideas looking for an exciting venture in an untapped market. Students at the graduate school of business are smart enough to learn how to create an impressive business plan, but sometimes, it's death by PowerPoint. Many are so gifted that they can sell it to investors and recruit their first employees. Sounds like a great start, but it's not. Instead, it's the reason we suspect that nine out of ten new companies that should work don't last.

Venture capitalist Ann Winblad, who has been investing in start-up companies for decades, notes that when the founders have rationalized a business plan that has nothing to do with their identity or what they deeply care about, "we won't touch that investment. For any start-up to succeed, they need every ounce of their heart, soul, and brains completely devoted to these ventures." When you skip the step of realizing what makes you tick, then you're taking the big risk that you've not landed on something upon which you can build success that will last.

Technology pundit and author, Esther Dyson, surfed the dot-com wave without crashing on the rocks. In addition to her writing, she invests in and coaches ventures during their earliest stages of development. She thinks an entrepreneur has to "have some feeling for it. When you're tone deaf, that means you can't pick up the music, and you can't pick up the music if you didn't grow up in that world," she said.

"Once I had a guy come to me [with] a really nice business plan all about building some kind of [online, virtual] community for families. He really understood how to make money off it and so forth. So I met him. And he was maybe 25. He was certainly an MBA. He clearly hadn't called his mother in about three years. He had absolutely no sense of family. And so I passed. He ended up not getting funded. And six months or nine months later, I heard that he was doing a start-up for college alumni. And that was perfect for him," Dyson said.

"But for a guy like that to do something for families, it just didn't resonate. It wasn't his thing. And it might have been a great plan, but it wasn't something he himself could really get into."

All too often, people launch grand plans without this vital link to personal meaning. Without an explicit understanding of their connection with a personal curiosity or passion that matters in their lives, the risk of terminal failure for the venture increases significantly—not to mention the added stress that can take years off the founder's life.

Built to Last revealed that a core ideology—in other words, a set of core values and an enduring purpose—beats most any great idea for building visionary companies. Collins' and Porras' research confirmed that starting out with ideological clarity matters even more than how good or bad the original product or service is!

The same holds true for your career and your life. If this seems like an "unreasonably" high standard, remember that most new ventures fail and life isn't fair. Builders have unreasonably high standards that give them the edge to last and prosper.

"The quest is for the story," said Barbara Waugh, author of *The Soul in the Computer*. "What story is worth your life?"

This may seem grandiose, and perhaps it is, but how much more of the rest of your life do you want to waste? Whether they're running a household or a company or a country, Builders come to the conclusion that doing something that matters to them is a dream worth their life.

Rational Optimism or Irrational Exuberance?

When a person finds something worth their life, like becoming a lover, what do they do? Many foolish things. But one of the most constructive compulsions is a tendency to focus on what's right about what and whom you love.

When you suppress your passion, you are teaching yourself to become a cynic. You're cynical because you care and don't want to risk getting hurt. On the other hand, lovers win because they are willing to take that risk for the right reasons. They are openly optimistic and grateful for the circumstances that helped make their experience possible.

Of course, you won't find many stories about that in fashionable magazines. Celebrating what's right with the world is an excruciatingly unhip and uncool thing to do. We are carefully trained by safety-conscious parents, in-laws, institutions of higher learning, and the evening news to ignore or ridicule optimistic people. In a world rife with violence and generally consumed by fight-or-flight—where most people teeter on the verge of being upset or angry—it's

> *Celebrating what's right with the world is an excruciatingly unhip and uncool thing to do. We are carefully trained by safety-conscious parents, in-laws, institutions of higher learning, and the evening news to ignore or ridicule optimistic people.*

hard for many people to function when they're not scared or worrying about something.

Optimism is a tough pill to swallow and seems a silly placebo at that. It presents an uneasy vacuum that feels unrealistic. Under these circumstances, it really seems there is no safe place in our society for boundless optimism.

As schoolyard bullies used to tell us, optimists are stupid. They are particularly irritating because they don't over-react to negative news or setbacks. They feel the fear and persist in doing things anyway and have the audacity to expect them to work. They actually believe that things will turn out well, that even if they don't at first, they will work out eventually, and that there are good people who will be served by whatever it is.

They are convinced that there are people who will want to sign up to make the dream a reality. Some would call it faith, but it's safer to dismiss this all as Pollyanna thinking and issue strong warning statements about how naïve and misguided it all might be.

Poet Maya Angelou found perspective on this attitude in her youth: "When complainers would come into the store, my grandmother would call me from wherever I was and say, 'Sister, come here and stand behind the counter.' She would say to the customer, 'How do you feel this morning, Mr. Shepard?' And the man would say, 'Oh, Sister Henderson, I hate the winter, I just hate it. It's cracking my skin, and I just can't get warm....' And my grandmother would say, 'Mm-hmm,' and then look at me with piercing eyes like, *'Did you hear that?'*"

"In the summer, another person would come in and mama would ask, 'How do you feel, Sister Williams?' and she would say 'Oh, I hate the summer, Sister Henderson. It hurts my scalp, makes me itch, and my skin....' And then when the person would leave, she would call me. She said, 'Sister, there are people all over the world who would give anything for just five minutes of what that person was complaining about.'"

Like Maya's grandmother, Builders tend to see the benefits of a situation rather than dwell on the negative. But here's the paradox about enduringly successful people—they're optimistic, pessimistic, and *irrationally exuberant*—a phrase favored by retired Federal Reserve Chairman Alan Greenspan to describe the dot-com bubble and real-estate markets when they reached what he considered speculative levels. The enthusiasm of Builders is huge, but not boundless. It's focused on what they want to build. If we were to measure optimism and pessimism on a scale, the needle would clearly weigh in the positive direction for successful people, but it's not that simple.

"I desperately struggled to stay focused and optimistic—it was really miserable after the awful events of September 11th," former New York City Mayor Rudy Giuliani told us over coffee at the Waldorf. "I couldn't tell people to 'be brave' unless I was willing to walk the streets myself. But the leader has to be optimistic simply because if he isn't, nobody else will be."

Optimists tend to see their successes as their own "fault"—they hold themselves accountable by way of their own talents and effort, as well as their special brand of serendipitous good luck. They see each success as long lasting and affecting everything in their lives.

Martin Seligman, one of the fathers of "positive psychology," calls this an *optimistic attributional (thought) style*. Pessimists tend to interpret any failure the same three ways that optimists see success: "pervasive, permanent, and personal," according to Seligman in his book, *Learned Optimism*. The next time you're faced with what you consider to be a success or failure, pay attention to how you come out on those three dimensions.

"The pessimist sees the difficulty in every opportunity," Abraham Lincoln said. "The optimist sees the opportunity in every difficulty." He should know. Abe Lincoln was a depressed fellow, according to Seligman, but he was able to talk himself through his darkest days. He had plenty of them, suffering failure after failure in his career before becoming president during the worst period in American history.

"I am an optimist," Winston Churchill is famously quoted. "It does not seem too much use being anything else." He fought depression, too. Lots of enduringly successful people suffer the dark side, the "shadow self," as some call it; some for their entire lives. It's important to note that the people we met, however, chose to use pessimistic behaviors selectively when the stakes were great.

The most notable place for pessimism, of course, is when the cost of failure is death. Builders use a more pessimistic attitude—for example, to slow down and "de-ice the plane one more time," said Southwest Airlines' founder Herb Kelleher. "We love to have fun. In fact, we require it." But, it's responsible optimism. Because the penalty is fatal, safety comes first.

Once you take death and taxes out of the equation, however, it's tougher to measure what is rational in terms of risk-taking and boundless enthusiasm. For successful people, risk-taking ranges from bet-it-all gambling by some entrepreneurs to conservative experimentation by others. You'll rarely see a frank admission that we really don't know what a reasonable risk was in any person's life, career, or company's development (short of death as an outcome).

Most financial planners, for example, will tell you to diversify your investments. The idea is to increase your chances that some of your investments will do well compared with the bad ones over the long haul so you have a better retirement.

Many millionaires did it that way. But it's also true that most billionaires did not diversify their portfolio on the way to super-wealth. Many put all their eggs in one basket. Chances are that their success has been described as a rational choice because it worked that time.

As Mark Twain said, "Everyone is a crank until their wild scheme actually works out." We'll never know how many entrepreneurs with the same risk profile and similar strategy entered bankruptcy.

Either way, we can be certain there were probably many skeptics and naysayers along the way (who are right most of the time), but not in the exceptional, once-desperate rags to riches cases of billionaires like Oprah Winfrey or J.K. Rowling, author of the *Harry Potter* series. After all, there are many more millionaires who diversified their risks than there are billionaires. We can only assume that the over-whelming majority of big risk-takers are eventually described as irrationally optimistic only after they crashed, burned, and vanished from the headlines.

We aren't suggesting either path. No one can tell you what risks you should take. We are insisting that you must choose a path that you love, for better or for worse, because only then will you have the good-hearted stubbornness to stretch for your full potential and survive the inevitable slings and arrows that await you on your bold journey.

> *No one can tell you what risks you should take. We are insisting that you must choose a path that you love, for better or for worse.*

You've got to love what you're doing or you can be sure there will be someone else who will. Falling in love, with all the rational and irrational exuberance that is involved, is the only way you have a prayer of creating success that lasts.

CHAPTER 3

Portfolio of Passions—
It's Not About Balance

It's exciting to see how fast your kids learn and grow. I'm not too worried about them, particularly the ones who like to break the rules and don't follow instructions; those are the ones that will do just fine because they know what's important to them.
—Michael Dell

To find your mission in life is to discover the intersection between your heart's deep gladness and the world's deep hunger.
—Frederick Beekner

The moment she heard the baby cry, she was compelled to do the same. What poor 16-year-old single mother wouldn't? Yet mingled with her desperation were the persistence, hope, and drive that would mark her path to eventual greatness.

Maya Angelou[1] would become the first bestselling African-American author (*I Know Why the Caged Bird Sings*),[2] one of the most popular living poets of our time, an Emmy Award-winning actress and producer, a university professor,[3] a mentor to Oprah Winfrey, a civil rights activist and Martin Luther King's protégé, and the first African-American woman admitted to the Directors Guild of America.

People hearing Maya read one of her poems at President Bill Clinton's inauguration in 1993 may know of her artistic achievements, but may not know that she was sexually assaulted at age eight by her mother's boyfriend; after which she turned silent for the next four years, refusing to speak to anyone but her brother. Nor could they know that to survive and support her young son, Guy, she had been a SF cable car operator, danced in night clubs, cooked at a Creole cafe, removed paint at a body shop, and even had been a madam in a San Diego brothel.

Angelou has come a long way from growing up in segregated Stamps, Arkansas, to where she is today. But, if there is a secret to her success, it was that she found many ways to feed her soul.

"You can't simply sit on the sidelines and bemoan one's outcast state; it's not enough," she told Mark Thompson over cookies and coffee in the living room of her Wake Forest home. "This experience, this life, is our one time to be ourselves."

> *"If I see something I don't like, I try to change it, and if can't change it, I change my position of looking at it, and then by seeing it from a different angle, I might be able to change it; or I might find some good in it that I can use, which might make it change itself.*

This isn't spin—spin denies accountability for creating what you want. As Angelou encounters resistance to her dreams, she responds the way many enduringly successful people do: She finds new ways to look at the issue. "If I see something I don't like, I try to change it, and if I can't change it, I change my position of looking at it, and then by seeing it from a different angle, I might be able to change it; or I might find some good in it that I can use, which might make it change itself. If you find that the world just won't work the way you want it to—if you can't make things happen despite your very best efforts—then change the way you look at it."

The Reward for the Doing Must Be the Doing

When asked if that viewpoint included an awareness of when she started to have impact on the world, she admonished that it's not healthy to think that way. "It's best not to do that. The reward for the doing must be the doing." When people tell her they love her work, she responds with only a simple, "Thank you." And when called a "liar or hack or worse—I've been called all those things—I say, 'Thank you.'" If she buys into the adulation, it would make her vulnerable to a focus on outside opinion—so when she hears harsh criticism, she would be vulnerable to that as well.

Neither the toxic nor the intoxicating influences of celebrity status are helpful in achieving your goals. Angelou feels they both threaten to distract from the creative work. "As the African proverb says, I don't pick that up; I don't lay that down. Because, if I were to pick up the one (the compliment), I have to pick up the other (the acrimony). And I still have my work to do!"[4]

Success can be the worst thing that happens to you if you think it makes you right. "Being right can make you righteous," Angelou said, and we often stop listening to how we can improve. Success as traditionally defined doesn't mean we're right; it just means that whatever happened turned out to be popular. You're bound to suffer rather than enjoy life if you rely on the public to tell you how to feel.

Angelou carved out an extraordinary career and created a life that has great personal meaning to her, with or without good reviews. At the same time, she has had lasting impact in the world. But it has not all been an upward spiral. She has also been penalized for her audacity to define her own version of success. Now in her late 70s, she continues to be the target of both contention and admiration, yet she remains hugely popular.

How does Maya remain so prolific and make success last? She said it's her *portfolio of passions*. Few people have excelled at so many different interests, but Angelou believes that if she didn't indulge in many of them, she might have none of them. For Angelou, there is dance, singing, acting, writing, teaching, literature, sunsets, April showers, good food, great friends—and the list goes on without obvious synergies.

Although one passion usually dominates Builders' lives and defines their successes in the eyes of the world, it's a mistake to believe there is just one passion that must be pursued at the expense of all others.

The Answer Is Very Rarely Just One Thing

In the movie *City Slickers*, Jack Pallance (Curly) told Billy Crystal (Mitch Robbins) the secret to life. Holding up one finger, he said as if speaking from the wisdom of the ages: "Just one thing."

Audiences felt terrific leaving the theatre with an answer, but this was fast food. It's just a fantasy that satisfies our compulsive need for a single magic pill for the happily ever after. But that kind of thinking is also the source of enormous frustration if you deny yourself everything else you've got going for you in life.

In organizations, it's often necessary to focus on one core competency—the one thing that your team is better at than others. And, in your career, a central focus to which you are willing to deeply commit is also important, as we'll explore later in this book. But, this focus should not be confused with a narrow life. Builders may look like race horses sprinting with blinders on, but most live large and complicated lives filled with many different personal and professional passions. The myth that there is only one thing to do with your life is not an idea that we could get many to endorse.

Balance Is Bullshit

Ironically, at the same time society insists that you do one thing with your life, those same cultural norms pressure you to have a "balanced" life split into neat little slices. That means not one, but at least four, miraculously proportioned commitments of time and mindshare. Again, the problem here is thinking there's a right answer—the notion that balance can be defined by a time allocation pie chart carrying the good housekeeping seal of approval, representing work, family, community, and if you're lucky, you're included in there somewhere, too.

> *Ironically, at the same time society insists that you do one thing with your life, those same cultural norms pressure you to have a "balanced" life split into neat little slices.*

When asked what he thought about life balance, Keith *Never-Eat-Alone* Ferrazzi didn't hold back: "Balance is bullshit!" he asserted. The voice in your head might reply, "Wrong answer." What do Builders have to say on the matter? Basically this: As culturally defined, balance is in fact bullshit—as a popular concept, it ranks right up there with the idea that there is just one passion for your life, and when you know what it is, you'll be happy. It rarely works this way.

If you define balance in the sense that it requires equal proportions of life partitioned into four or five politically correct parts, then CEOs and presidents don't have balance, nor do most Nobel laureates. The Dalai Lama doesn't either, nor does Nelson Mandela or Bono. Martin Luther King, Jr., and Mother Teresa did not have balance—we could go on and on, but you get the idea. Enduringly successful people, many of whom live a life that's a gift to the world, don't raise balance as a major issue—not because they had it masterfully handled, but because they were all busy doing what mattered to them.

It's a struggle for everyone at some point. If you're feeling a twinge of guilt about balance, there is a probability that you don't want more balance, exactly, but need more of something that you can't admit you want. The balance you're seeking is a meaningful portfolio, not a balanced one. The reason that balance is so painful and elusive is because that's not what you really want. What you hunger for is a place for all of your passions—not balance as culturally defined.

Feeling a desperate need for balance may have nothing to do with balance *per se* as much as it means "you're not getting access to a huge chunk of time to do the things that really matter to you," said Gordon Moore, co-founder of Intel and best known for *Moore's Law*. In addition to his love for crunching numbers and inventing technology in Silicon Valley, this big-hearted, down-to-earth billionaire has many other passions that he ferociously pursues, such as philanthropy, sport fishing, education, and saving the planet. Your fixation on balance may actually mean you need your work 80%, or kids 80%, or fishing 80%, but rarely in "comfortable" proportions. It might mean time to be a stay-at-home parent, refurbish Model Ts without the family around, explore medieval castles with your pals, or paint homes for Habitat for Humanity.

The point is to look and see if it's a neglected passion that drives the hunger, not a social obligation to some idealistic sense of balance. When you say to yourself you need more balance, ask yourself: if you had it, what would you be doing that you're not doing now? Chances are a neglected passion is making the request. Pay attention. What you really need is to balance your portfolio of passions. Understand that what you will actually experience as balance can change with the passage of time and may never look like balance to any other soul.

You don't have to make a career of everything that is meaningful to you, but you do need to find a place for everything that is meaningful to you. That's the balance that you are seeking.

> *You don't have to make a career of everything that is meaningful to you, but you do need to find a place for everything that is meaningful to you. That's the balance that you are seeking.*

Endowing Others with a Portfolio of Passions

On the way to lasting success and a life that matters, Builders embrace more than one passion and sometimes their passion becomes to endow others with their own portfolios. As a tenth grader living in inner-city Pittsburg, Bill Strickland saw dreams shattered daily and he felt a deep need to do something to get and give hope where there was none.

One day, he was walking past a classroom and something caught his eye that stopped him in his tracks. To hear him tell it, "—time stopped. It was a Wednesday afternoon and I was minding my own business and the door of the art room happened to be open, and I happened to look in. And there was this teacher named Frank Ross making a great big old ceramic bowl. I just stood there transfixed." It was like magic for him. Bill fell in love with ceramics, but the metaphor changed his life and tens of thousands of other at-risk kids and adults. As CEO of Manchester Bidwell Corporation and the Bidwell Training Center, he has created extensive training programs and facilities in a world-class architectural setting where his passion for art feeds his passion for building a stronger community.

"Mothers and fathers instinctively know that the arts are the basis of good mental health and good intellectual development. When children are born, the mothers and fathers have them doing rhyming, they have them doing clapping, they have them singing, and they have them using crayons. All these creative things, instinctively, we know are the basis for good human development. When kids are 5 years old we take it away from them and we wonder why the kids are nuts 20 years later. My theory is that we need the arts as a part of our mental health."

Obviously, the arts are not the only passions you can use to enrich your life, but they have served as Strickland's unique way to give those in poverty the opportunity to believe in themselves and trust their portfolios of passions.

"You don't have to live a life of mediocrity; you don't have to live a life that has no positive outcome." If there is any such thing as balance, he said, art "is essential to the way that you create balance in life. The arts contribute to that part of the human vocabulary. And you take it away from people and it makes them sick."

Your Passions Provide Peripheral Vision

When you take a timeout to shift your attention from the stressful stuff to something uplifting and apparently unrelated—particularly if it's one of your passions—your state of mind improves. Enduringly successful people find they get many great insights when they're playing at something else—or somehow not wrestling with problems directly. Don't shortchange the subtle power that comes from purposely changing the subject of your attention in the middle of the week.

It's like peripheral vision, enabling you to see more angles on an idea or new dimensions of an issue when you're not looking directly at it. This may seem nonintuitive or odd, yet we all have these experiences—ideas that show up in the shower, or while we're pushing a child on the swing, playing a favorite game, or daydreaming during a long drive. As long as there is a connection to your portfolio of passions rather than just a focus on obligations or an attempted escape in wishful thinking, you can take advantage of what we call, peripheral thinking. *Peripheral thinking* has the potential to connect you with a higher authority. Many people have creative breakthroughs (a.k.a. *Aha!* moments) in prayer, or meditation, or even playing basketball.

"I love the game," said lanky, athletic-looking Richard Kovacevich, who takes this principle to heart in his life and work. He said he has always been at his best when he applies what he learned on the basketball court to his day job as president, chairman, and CEO of Wells Fargo & Company. Kovacevich is one of the most respected leaders in business at one of the most successful financial services companies in the world.

"I've made every mistake there is in life as a manager," he said. "I was an engineer by background, although I got an MBA, but I have an MS in engineering. And as an engineer, I thought, just sit in a room with my slide rule and just run your linear program and the answer would pop out. Then just send the answer to the troops telling them what to do and it would get done. Well, in my first real job, I did all that and nothing happened," he said. He tried that a few times. "And they nodded and said 'Yes,' and it still didn't happen. And then I said, 'Well gee, this is not working too well, is it?' And so you learn. And what you really find out is it's all about people. Although I was this geek, this engineer, I also spent four hours every day of my life for 21 years playing sports. You learn very quickly playing sports that it's all about (the) team. It's the best five players that win the basketball game, not the five best players. I learned more on the field of sports than I did in my calculus class. And you start applying those types of experiences, combined with business knowledge and you say, 'Wow, this is what it's all about.'"

Stealth Passions and the Power of Peripheral Thinking

Another potential payoff from experimenting with peripheral thinking is that it might unlock a passion that is your secret talent or even a new specialty you've been unable or unwilling to reveal until a collection of passions all came colliding together—giving you a peek at what you'd rather be doing when the world isn't watching and not requiring you to pay bills. If at first you don't pressure yourself to take them too seriously—but do them anyway—a portfolio of passions may give you a unique opportunity to look honestly at things that you care about without your harshest critic—yourself—judging or dismissing what matters to you.

It's common knowledge that it requires focus to achieve a specific objective. But blind pursuit of just one thing is like searching for El Dorado. When you exclude all other things except a single focus for your life, there is a danger that you might find it impossible to locate the real treasure. Single-mindedness forces you to sideline passions that, with further development, could come together as your genius or eventually become your organization's core greatness.

We are not suggesting that you abandon all plans, scatter your efforts to the four winds, and become a wandering philosopher. It's just that being creative in your passions has a place in your life and work, with benefits that can't be forced or predicted. Peripheral thinking has the potential to catalyze a chemical reaction waiting within you—a set of passions that could move the world we share in the direction of goodness. Honor that part of yourself. Carve out a little time each week, on the job or after work, to experiment in some way with one of your other passions.

> *Carve out a little time each week, on the job or after work, to experiment in some way with one of your other passions.*

Bill Nye's career unfolded exactly that way. When we met him in his office near the Seattle Space Needle, it was hard to find a place to sit down among all the whiz-bang scientific toys. Bill's eyes sparkled as he scooped up a bright, shiny ball and plopped it into the top of an elaborate towering maze, where it clanged and banged its way on a circuitous route to the bottom. "You could live without this, but why would you want to?" he quipped, an expression he used to describe each of his wild gadgets as if it was show-and-tell time in the classroom. These things embodied the eclectic combination of Nye's three passions: education, science, and humor. Nye was the kind of kid fascinated with how things worked. Every week, you could find him pulling apart every bicycle he could find, and rumor has it he got most of them back together. He was also intrigued with the ways people learn. His mother had a Ph.D. in education, and he found himself tutoring other kids in school, spreading his love of math and science. He majored in mechanical engineering at Cornell University and took a job at Boeing International designing airplanes.

Then, Nye decided to try his hand at a core competency that wasn't acceptable in the office at that time—comedy. He entered a Steve Martin "look alike" contest and won even though he doesn't look anything remotely like Martin. It was his deep scientific understanding of Martin's sick humor that took the prize, Nye claimed. He also started doing stand-up at comedy clubs and moonlighting on a Seattle-based TV show called *Almost Live*.

In his spare time, he volunteered tutoring kids struggling with math and science and gave presentations to kids at the Pacific Science Center, teaching the basic principles of science—"like how to blow liquid nitrogen smoke out your nose," he said. "Don't try this at home!" he sagely advised. "You've got to put in the hours to pull this stunt off safely."

For years, he had wanted to do a TV show that would combine his love for education, science, and silliness, but even his friends told him he was nuts. Even he admits that it was nuts—it had never been successfully done before—but he didn't see why that should stop him from trying. Nye decided to reset the priority of his passions, "Or, dare I say it? *Change the world*," he exclaimed with a laugh. He quit his day job and accepted a part-time role doing engineering that would help underwrite his new full-time position writing comedy. He got grants from the Department of Energy and the National Science Foundation, and gathered a creative group of friends—the kind of pals he was so close to that they even share their most intimate toys, "like telescopes." As a result, the TV show, *Bill Nye The Science Guy*, was born. It ended up becoming a 100-part TV series that won 28 Emmys, influenced thousands of children, and is still distributed by Disney today. Now that Nye has three passions compressed into one career, what would be his ultimate achievement? "If one of the kids who watched the show would find a cure for cancer," Nye said, pausing a moment, "that would be pretty cool."

Where You Can Be Paid For Passionate Distractions

Firms like Google actually encourage employees to spend 15–20% of their time in this kind of unfocused discovery, despite how messy it may seem. Rather than having people moonlight at home in stealth mode, where the idea may die from neglect or take root so well that they choose to leave to do a start-up, the 20% rule is a way to encourage and support breakthrough ideas. People can take ownership of something they're inventing on one day a week or pool the days and take a few weeks.

The paid time underwrites employees as if they were entrepreneurial CEOs launching their own projects, like start-up companies, until the day it's ripe enough to show to management. Krishna Barat, principal scientist at Google, came up with *Google News* just this way. His personal interest in the media and his memories of listening to the BBC with his grandfather, back in India, were galvanized on 9/11, when the scramble to find news about the events of the day made it particularly obvious how hard it was to find and difficult to sort. When CEO Eric Schmidt dropped by to give him the thumbs up, and founders Larry Page and Sergey Brin gave their endorsement, Barat's dream became a full-time endeavor.

Unfortunately, the perceived reality for most people is that you've got to keep your head down to the tasks of your job. As a practical matter, you may feel you don't have the money, time, or energy to take a side trip to explore a potential passion, particularly if your company won't offer support. If you are like most people, you have to work to pay for housing and care for loved ones, and you put other passions on the back burner until the day that other critical needs or goals are met. As you most likely already know, of course, those very same concerns and limitations were also real and threatening for the vast majority of entrepreneurs and enduringly successful people. They felt the fear and did it anyway. Few passions come conveniently prefinanced; you have to pay for them with sweat equity whenever you can squeeze them in.

"We must test our fantasies—otherwise, they remain just that," said Herminia Ibarra. "Either the fantasy never finds a match in the real world, paycheck-producing job or," she warned, you "remain emotionally attached to a fantasy career that you do not realize you have outgrown—while you wait for the flash of blinding insight, opportunities pass you by. To launch ourselves anew, we need to get out of our heads. We need to act. We learn who we have become—in practice, not in theory—by testing fantasy and reality, not by 'looking inside.' Knowing oneself is crucial, but it is usually the outcome of—and not a first input to—the reinvention process," she said. "I discovered that most people create new working identities on the side at first, by getting involved in extracurricular ventures and weekend projects—the only way we figure out what we really want to do is by giving it a try."[5]

Transforming Lives for 64 Cents Apiece

In Chittagong, Bangladesh, 14 children were born one after another to the owners of a small Muslim ornament store during the 1930s and '40s. As was common in this part of the world, five of the children perished before age 5.

As a young teen, Muhammad Yunus, the third of the remaining nine children, took a pilgrimage thousands of miles from Bangladesh, through India, to the First Pakistan National Boy Scout Jamboree. It changed the 13-year-old's life, seeding (or more likely, revealing) three very different passions that at the time were strange bedfellows. They would define his life's legacy: social work, education, and economics.

Yunus loved economics and received a Fulbright Scholarship to dive into it completely, and within the next few years, he earned a Ph.D. and became a professor in the United States.

At 32, he returned home to Bangladesh and landed a government job shortly after the country won its independence from Pakistan.[6] He was bored to tears, but an epic tragedy would change his life again.

In 1974, devastating floods killed more than ten times the number of people as the 2004 tsunami—over 1.5 million people died in Bangladesh. During the time, this already poorest of poor nations struggled to recover, Yunus conceived the notion of "micro-lending"—the Grameen Bank Project—which defied traditional banking rules.

From Begging Bowls to Cash Boxes

"Think about what it means to sit with a mother who, after toiling all day on making a bamboo stool, has enough only to starve with her children," he said, sipping hot tea. Like her parents before her, she was forced to pay off local bullies and brokers like an indentured serf, leaving her just pennies per chair on which to subsist.

He sought out every person in the village of Jobra who lived like this, and met 42 families in "horrible suffering." In 1976, he gave unsecured loans—with no collateral and no credit history—to each of them. Yunus loaned a total of $27—about 64 cents each was all it took to lift them from starvation to the first steps toward transformation. The small loans were enough to enable the villagers to start small businesses and sell their own special products.

By 2005, Grameen Bank had invested almost $5 billion in millions of families. Yunus' now famous "dream was to turn begging bowls into cash boxes." Yunus turned his many different passions into one compelling mission that has also spawned similar programs the world over, from Harlem to Sri Lanka.

The Paranoid Survive, But the Passionate Prosper

No stranger to controversy, Paul Hewson built two of his passions into dual careers that have brought him fame and a sort of infamy.

First, we have to admit we didn't recognize this Builder when we first met, nor did we know his music or his social activism when we ran into him accidentally in New York. We were standing there talking about our spouses at the World Economic Forum when this sort of short, shaggy Irish-sounding bloke burst into the conversation wearing see-through sunglasses that rock star wannabes often wear. He bragged that he had married his high school sweetheart, Alison "Ali" Stewart, with whom he was still married and had four children.

After a few moments, it was clear that the joke was on us. This was Bono, as Paul Hewson is affectionately known, erupting with infectious enthusiasm and playful banter that would steal the show, even though we were standing there chatting before a press conference he was about to have with Bill Gates. As it turned out, the new millennium's odd couple of philanthropic activism, Gates and Bono, were there to announce their latest HIV initiative.

Three decades ago, Bono saw an ad to form a band that, after the usual artistic fits and starts, eventually boiled down to enormously popular U2. In his music and his social activism, Bono takes on the biggest of issues: love and hate, life and death, power and politics.

Today, he faces criticism about whether his main love, music, and his second passion, social activism, might both be losing their progressive edginess in favor of self-promotion or political correctness in deference to his growing circle of rich, famous, and powerful friends.

"Aren't you sleeping with the enemy?" Some anonymous bystander took a cheap shot as we walked quickly down the hall, late for another meeting. The joust was in reference to Bono's high-profile hobnobbing with the suits, crashing on Bill Gates' couch or holding court with Presidents Bush and Clinton.

Bono ignored the provocation, and then attacked as if we had started the argument.

"Do you really want these ideas to die?" he snapped. "It's an everyday holocaust.[7] Twenty-five million Africans who are HIV-positive will leave behind 40 million AIDS orphans by the end of the decade." He stopped for a moment in the hallway. His temperature dropped as he sighed, turning from adversary to recruiter. "It's time we all got a bloody grip on this, don't you think? It's pathetic, gutless really. It doesn't have to be this way. We can do something about this."

Bono, along with his pals, Bill and Melinda Gates, were named *Time Magazine's 2005 Persons of the Year* for their extraordinary alliance in rallying otherwise adversarial economic and political powers to have an actual impact on global social issues.

For Builders, Every Passion Counts

Wealthy people have been giving piles of money away to good causes for generations. Some of it makes a difference and some doesn't. But it is obvious when you sit down with Gates and Bono that having impact has always been as big a passion as philanthropy has become for them. But whether they are sitting on the mud floor in a hut in Africa or sipping champagne with the rich and famous in Washington D.C., Gates and Bono know how to work the system in government and business.

"It's an amazing thing to think that ours is the first generation that really can end extreme poverty...[but] we let our own pathetic excuses about how it's 'difficult' to [make social change really happen] to justify our own inaction," Bono told the World Association of Reporters, entreating the media and public to get with the program. "Be honest. We have the science, the technology, and the wealth. What we don't have is the will, and that's not a reason that history will accept."[8]

History will honor the many passions of physician and storyteller, Rachel Naomi Remen. "I was the only premed in preschool," she said. Remen is one of the few people we met who was blessed with knowing what her profession would be early in life, but her ideas about medicine and healing were unconventional.

"Because of my own experience with chronic illness, I knew that there was more to the healing of disease than the curing of the body. That there might be a relationship between the mind and the body, and this was seen as absurd." In 1972, as a young doctor at Stanford Medical School, Remen had studied at Esalen on the California coast—a center of the emerging Human Potential movement—where many of these ideas became woven into her thinking about illness.

Dr. Remen's course, *The Healer's Art*, is now taught by more than 200 faculty in 46 medical schools. Her books are widely read by health professionals and the public and have been translated into 13 languages. She is an internationally recognized teacher, physician, and counselor to physicians and the cancer patients they treat. Her work was featured in the ground-breaking Bill Moyer's PBS television series, *Healing and the Mind*. Her books, *Kitchen Table Wisdom: Stories That Heal* and *My Grandfather's Blessings: Stories of Strength, Refuge, and Belonging*, are enduring bestsellers. Many thousands of people have been guided in their healing and their healing work by her writings and her example.

But, decades ago, she was ridiculed for her insights about medicine. "The first time I presented at Grand Rounds, I talked about a healthy way to have a disease and the possibility that you can lead a good life even though it wasn't an easy life. I presented the case histories of patients who through the experience of suffering had become deeper, larger, wiser human beings and suggested that this might become a part of our goal as physicians. There were 400 doctors in the room. By the time I had finished talking, three-quarters of them had left."

How did she feel about the rejection?

"In a funny way, it didn't matter," she mused. "What mattered is that a quarter of the doctors were still in the room. You know, vision is never established by a majority vote."

Remen is one of the cofounders of the Commonweal Cancer Help Program, one of the first residential support retreats for people with cancer. "I think one of the most important lessons that I have learned from working with people with cancer is that people are able to use some of the most difficult experiences in life in order to learn how to live better and help the people around them to live better."

Leaders Give What Is Needed, Not What Is Expected

Often, leaders do not recognize their potential for leadership, especially when they are young, Remen said. They may have a portfolio of passions that don't neatly fit together. "Their experience is an experience of difference—that they don't belong, that somehow or other they're a square peg in a round hole or they don't fit in, and this can be very painful and lonely. Occasionally, a medical student will tell me that they don't fit in, that they feel so out of place in today's medicine that they are considering dropping out. I encourage them to stop trying to fit in because the medicine that they will fit into has not happened yet. It is part of the future. They will never find the medicine that fits for them, they will have to build it. And when they build it for themselves they will build it for all the rest of us, too.

"Many of the world's great leaders were considered neither great, nor even leaders in their day. Passion is what enables leaders to hold to their integrity despite social pressures," said Remen. "Real leaders were born to do what they are doing. They may have not known that when they were young, but there is an inner guidance system that makes them perfect for their time and the unmet needs of their culture.

"Leaders are people who don't compromise their values to gain approval, who live up to their own inner sense of things. And for this reason, leadership is often different than success. Success is culturally defined. When you give the culture what it expects, the culture will reward that. But, a leader is someone who gives the culture what it needs, not what it expects," Remen contended. "A real leader heals the wounds of their culture," she said.

"Many of the world's leaders, in their own time, were not respected, were not seen as successful people, and in retrospect, they served us all." Builders like Remen, Gates, and Bono have been relentless at sticking with what has mattered to them in their lives, and they've always found it particularly appetizing if the issue they're pursuing had something to do with messing with conventional wisdom about how things have been done for millennia.

That kind of conviction magnetizes support in amazing ways. The world's second richest person, Warren Buffett, handed over his fortune to the world's richest couple to get something done that he had hoped his late wife would do had she survived: make a difference with their billions and make a statement doing it. For Buffett, being an investor "is so much fun that I'll never retire," but he also insists that his legacy serve social causes rather than make his kids crazy. He is convinced that Melinda and Bill Gates will get the job done. Is it any surprise that Bill Gates and Bono have grown in their effectiveness as social activists when their personal portfolios of passions include Melinda Gates and Ali Stewart? These women are steadfast philanthropists rather than self-absorbed royalty and, in critically important ways, have shown their spouses the path. For many Builders, their portfolio of passions launched them like juggernauts on historic missions that are a far cry from their beginnings—missions to get things done in parts of the world where things haven't gotten better for generations. For Builders, there is not just one thing to do with their life. Every passion counts.

Why Successful People Stay
Successful—Integrity to Meaning

The purpose of life is not to be happy. It is to be useful, to be honorable, to be compassionate, to have it make some difference that you have lived and lived well.
—Ralph Waldo Emerson

Rugby can be brutal. He heard a ghastly scream and for a split second thought that someone else was hurt, until he realized it was him. He could feel his knee joint tearing apart. A terrible pain spread throughout his leg as he rolled in agonized slow motion on the field. It was now impossible to move. All his future plans imploded.

Struggling with dyslexia for years, it had become painfully obvious to Rickie that he would be lucky to graduate from high school. So, like many kids who suffer academic humiliation, he had hoped to go to college on an athletic scholarship. But now, these were broken dreams, and that hurt more than his knee.

He did manage to get back on his feet, but Rickie would never go to college. As he battled toward a high school diploma, his headmaster said, "I predict that you will either go to prison or become a millionaire." (He was, in fact, briefly imprisoned for dodging customs selling records.) Rickie reconsidered what really mattered to him, which helped him change the way he thought about his circumstances. He loved rock music and partying, so with boundless enthusiasm, he dedicated most of the next two decades to becoming an expert in both. Although unable to learn to write particularly well, this dyslexic 16-year-old dropped out of school in 1968 and started a British magazine ironically called *Student*. He went begging for interviews and recruited volunteer writers, who were, naturally, looking for any excuse to hang out with rock stars and to possibly get stoned with them.

Without money for an office for this motley crew, Rickie finally settled on what he could afford: a rent-free crypt where the tombs became makeshift desks. The creepiness of the place wore off quickly, as his passion for entertainment, wild parties, and building relationships around music launched his team onto the bleeding edge of pop culture. What had been a behavior problem in high school had become his genius as a shameless promoter.

He had learned to use his dyslexia as an asset: forcing any new ideas to be made compellingly simple so he could decode them. Rickie honed his special gift as he cut through the dull clutter of conventional thinking to create mesmerizing marketing memes and politically incorrect hype.

At 20, he founded a mail-order record company, then a record shop and a recording studio—all under the name of Virgin. Richard Branson had become a man whose name was synonymous with the hippest musical acts, ones that alarmed the old guard media sufficiently to generate mega demand from UK youth, but were just short of being completely banned by the authorities. Branson's Virgin brands would take the world by storm.

The last time Mark Thompson spoke with him, Mark was just finishing a favorite jog around Belvedere Island in San Francisco Bay when his cell phone rang.

"Could you hold for a moment, sir," the unknown voice said, "Mr. Branson is at the other end of the yacht and he asked me to get you on the line." Thompson guzzled Gatorade.

"Mark, this is Richard Branson. We met a few months ago in LA," he reminded. The previous meeting had taken place on one of those broken-down, moth-eaten couches that are standard issue in convention center green rooms you hang out in before giving a speech.

"Did I catch you at a bad time?" Branson continued. Thompson was still panting from his run. "Sounds like you're having even more fun than I am."

Branson was sailing with his wife and children in the waters of the Caribbean. Back in the 1980s, he had tearfully sold raucous Virgin Music to raise cash for new ambitions like Virgin Atlantic and a growing constellation of companies driven by his branding genius. Branson continues to fancy himself a sort of populist David versus entrenched, monopolistic Goliath brands that he believes fail to deliver on their promises to consumers.

Whether it's British Airways, Coca-Cola, or NASA, whenever the old guard takes its eye off the prize in almost any category, he feels a moral obligation to the public to set the big guy's platform on fire. His Sex Pistols are long gone, but his sense of outrageous adventure and iconoclastic headlines that challenge conventional wisdom will never die, whether it's the soft porn advertising of Virgin Atlantic in your hotel room or a new race for space.

But that's not why he was calling that day. He was excited about the new Virgin-branded mobile phone with a novel spin for youth—prepaid minutes. You might be imagining a high-energy pitchman, but in fact his quiet, warm personal style is disarmingly the opposite. He remembered from a brief chat five months earlier that Thompson had done extensive consulting with consumer retailers, and Branson was personally looking for every inroad to put his phones in retail stores.

This is a fellow who does not need to work a single day ever again. But here he was—on the job—scouring his network to get his next idea launched. Sir Richard was doing business while on vacation with his family—calling to pitch his product after hours when you would think he would be well past having to do that sort of thing in his life.

You have to admire a billionaire like that. Of the hundreds of people interviewed for *Success Built to Last*, more than a dozen are billionaires and all are still on the job today, working with the same intensity as ever. You have to wonder what it is about these people that keep them so passionately involved even after we might think they have long since "arrived" and no longer need to be working so hard.

Don't Treat Passion Like a Trivial Pursuit

For a couple of them, wealth was a good enough reason to work and seemed another way to keep score, but even then, it was rarely their focus. It never undermined their fierce determination to build something for its own sake. Their endeavors are not things from which these remarkable people can ever fully retreat or retire. That's why they stay successful for so long. To ask them why they're still "working" is to dismiss their passions as trivial pursuits. We made that mistake more than once in our interviews. It seemed an innocent question, but only served to demonstrate that we didn't get it.

> To ask them why they're still "working" is to dismiss their passions as trivial pursuits. We made that mistake more than once in our interviews. It seemed an innocent question, but only served to demonstrate that we didn't get it.

You might as well ask him why he wanted to "stay alive," Amazon founder Jeff Bezos said, squirming as if wondering how he got stuck sitting next to us at one of those two-hour talkfest dinners in Davos. "You're looking at my life in the rearview mirror!" he boomed with his trademark guffaw. His good-humored exterior is matched with a fiercely determined and analytical interior. Bezos said he didn't jump into his venture with an exit strategy that included a retirement plan. He wanted to revolutionize how retail business is done.

Bezos' net worth soared well north of $10 billion in 1999, when he found himself on the cover of *Time* as *Person of the Year*. Back then, he would say that he was trying to build a new way of doing business, "but we (Amazon) have so far to go." When the dot-com hysteria collapsed, it looked as if his fortune would go with it. That did not crush his boundless optimism. He was determined to build that business that he believed in, and like so many who failed before him, he wasn't going to give up.

Today, his dream is obviously working and his billions look more secure. But it's the former that matters, not the latter; and he still thinks he has a lot of work to do to realize his vision.

To wonder aloud why Builders keep building and stay so engaged after all these years is heard as an absurd question that misses the point of their lives—it's almost insulting, lacking serious consideration for the depth of feelings they have for what they care about. We shouldn't lose any sleep worrying about billionaires, of course; they can take care of themselves.

The problem is that, if what they've accomplished looks to you like they've landed on *Fantasy Island*, you'll find attempting to steal their treasure map an exercise in self-destruction. The real message is to take your intrusive and persistent dreams more seriously. Builders haven't been working this hard this long to win a prize to go sit on a beach and stop doing what has mattered to them all along. There is no destination for them. Their passions create meaning in their lives that is nothing short of lifelong obsession from which they seek no escape.

One Value That Builders Have in Common

People become fascinated by the lifestyles of the rich and famous, perhaps longing for the adulation, glamour, and imagined self-satisfaction in those lives. It may be tempting to believe you can find success by studying their stories and assuming that whatever she or he did is a roadmap you can follow. But that's a dead end. That's not what billionaires or the best CEOs do. That's not what heroes like Mother Teresa or Mahatma Gandhi did. That's not what the world's enduringly successful people do.

If there is one thing they all do consistently—one value that they all share in common—it is integrity to what matters to them. It is integrity to what they believe will make a difference. Whenever they are faced with a decision, they look to find meaning in that opportunity that is very personal to them. They do not waste their time if it doesn't matter.

> *If there was one thing they all do consistently— one value that they all share in common— it is integrity to what matters to them.*

It may seem odd to consider Branson in this context; however, there is significant evidence that he actually has values. Steadfast integrity to his unique sense of personal meaning has always been one of those values. His other values and passions include taking risks and "not being afraid to try new things," which is an understatement for a guy who has lived on the edge more than once in his life. He believes in loyalty to people he knows and trusts. He's passionate about toppling big brand monopolies that he contends "rip people off," and he is frequently heard proclaiming that "not taking yourself too seriously," "keeping things simple," and "having fun" are core values that should become your core competencies.

Many people admire him for his achievements; others think he's outrageous or worse. Either way, it's unlikely that many people have much in common with Sir Richard's particular talents and life experiences. You can, however, learn a lesson or two from him about finding meaning and building something that matters using creative thought and effective action.

Once upon a time, Branson was just another teen with a shattered dream and dim prospects, yet he continued thinking expansively about his options, thinking that it was up to him to create a future that mattered to him. If Branson was born in this millennium and subjected to the delusions of political correctness, he would likely be branded as a special-needs child. Good, well-intentioned people would speed his adaptation to the world of normal (read *average*) folks. His dyslexia and physical wounds would be contextualized as a reason for below-average achievement, rather than, as Branson actually used them, building blocks for an extraordinary life.

Richard Branson's obsession with simple and often outrageous ideas have given his marketing the power to cut through the clutter of competition and make things compelling and memorable. "How can I expect other people to get it if I don't? The good thing about being dyslexic is I need everything simplified for me," he said. "By simplifying everything and making things work for (even) me, I can then make it clear to other people."

Whatever their circumstances, Builders are consistent about one thing: They are always driving for meaning that makes a difference in their lives and work. Even Branson's *passions* and *pain* offer one example, although you might not otherwise consider embracing him as a role model.

In 30 years of working with teams in organizations to help them improve performance, we've routinely done what most every executive coach does: a determine-your-core-values exercise. The idea is to compare what you do with what you say. The exercise often reveals a big gap, but the problem is much more troubling than may, at first, be apparent. In these sessions, most people seem to come up with the list of values they think they should have to finish the assignment and look good. Worse yet, we do similar exercises with management teams who will then foist those values on their organizations as gospel.

Management teams without vision will invent mission statements for their employees, who in turn become cynical when the obvious "don't walk the talk" realities mark the words as empty platitudes.[1] The research for *Built to Last* revealed that visionary companies must have a set of core values that drive their decisions and actions, but there is not just one right set of values that work for every company.[2]

Neither individuals, nor organizations, as we learned in *Built to Last*, can "*create* or *set* core ideology. You discover core ideology. It is not derived by looking to the external environment; you get at it by looking inside. It has to be authentic. You can't fake an ideology. Nor can you 'intellectualize' it. Do not ask, 'What core values should we hold?' Ask instead: 'What core values do we actually hold?' Core values and purpose must be passionately held on a gut level or they are not core. Values you think the organization 'ought' to have, but that you cannot honestly say that it does have, should not be mixed into the authentic core values."[3] To do so creates a horrible backlash as much for a company as does it you as a human being.

There is perhaps not a more exaggerated arena of life than politics to make the point about how values can be interpreted as differently as night and day and yet still endure. The American people, for example, consistently vote for candidates based on a shared sense of values, not the least of which is the one that Builders hold so dear: integrity to what matters to them. But it's hard to imagine more divergent definitions of what that means than how the

Democratic and Republican leadership in the United States apply them.

Evaluating values is, gratefully, beyond the scope of this book. Our message is that lasting impact and your commitment to integrity (to personal meaning) as a core value go hand in hand. This core value is no less optional for you than it was for Kennedy, Carter, Reagan, Bush Sr., Clinton, and George W.—to name just a few recent American presidents—who arguably achieved political success for decades in their careers regardless of how we may judge their legacies. Hundreds of millions of Americans love them or hate them. Although they may have borrowed tactics from each other's playbooks at some point or another, none of these leaders followed the other's roadmap, nor did they choose to define their values or what mattered to them in exactly the same way as their predecessors—not even father and son.

It's not difficult to argue that these six presidents are remarkably different from each other, whether you consider values, character, personality, or contradictory priorities. It's amazing they shared enough appeal to hold the same job. They were men with a deep sense of purpose and mission, but the details were certainly different.

Although their core ideologies varied between each other, they rarely changed—even though the paths they took inevitably did. Carter and Reagan enjoyed two 20-year careers during the course of each of their extraordinary lifetimes. They built their own personal definitions of success, and then reinvented them during two chapters of their lives.

During Ronald Reagan's second term as governor of California, he met with a group of high school students on a field trip in Sacramento. Reagan told them that when he was in high school, he was better known for his beauty than his brains. "I was a C student who worked his tail off to become a B actor," he quipped. As a teen, he wasn't sure he was up to the task of memorizing a movie script, let alone understanding government.

His abilities in both careers have long been the subject of great admiration and derision. But his 53 films over two decades were followed by one of the most influential careers in political history. Reagan was never lacking clarity about the one value that Builders share: integrity to what mattered to him. He claimed his own definition of success and two long, rewarding careers that had lasting, though not equal, impact.

His predecessor, Jimmy Carter, was crushed in a landslide as Reagan swept into office in the 1980 presidential election. It was a very public humiliation. And, like Reagan, he also had great clarity about his values and what he believed he must do, which helped him achieve two decades of success in his first career. Here, we have another impossible story that has become legend.

Jimmy Carter grew up in relative isolation outside Plains, Georgia, a community of 500 with only "black playmates in an era of total racial segregation—during the Great Depression years, when the more affluent people around us, who were sharecroppers, had an annual income of $75," he told us during an interview at the Carter Center. No one in his family had ever finished high school before—and this fellow goes to college to study nuclear physics, jumps into politics, and ends up the 39th President of the United States. He would have to reinvent his definition of success, however, after his first term.

"When I left the White House, I was in despair," Carter said. "I had not anticipated being defeated after the first term. I had put everything I owned—a very successful business—in a blind trust—I found that during the four years I was in the White House, I had accumulated a debt of a million dollars; I had no way to pay it off." He was going to move back to Georgia, but "there were no job opportunities there."

When he was essentially thrown out at the end of his first term, he suffered a deep depression. "I think everybody has to be prepared in life for failures or disappointments or frustrated dreams, or even embarrassments," he said. "We have to be prepared to accommodate them if possible. You have to accommodate changing times but cling to unchanging principles. If you do have an extreme change in your life that is unpleasant, what are the principles that don't change, on which you can build a new life, an expanded life, a better life, a more adventurous life?"

"In my case, it was a stable family, a community from which I came, but primarily my religious faith. I teach in my little church every Sunday—the preeminent facets of which are selfless love, compassion, forgiveness, justice, humility, service. That's a perfect description of a successful person in the eyes of God. None of us can measure up to that perfection. But, I would say, in the most dismal times of life, this can be a strong enough inspiration to overcome despair and disappointment and failure. Each of us has to struggle in our own individual way to achieve a measurement of success."

"Each of us has to struggle in our own individual way to achieve a measurement of success."

Carter decided "to use whatever talents or ability or influence that my wife and I had—having been president, First Family—to get to know the rest of the world and to address the problems of some of the people who had really not been on my top priority—or even my medium priority— while I was president. When you are president, you have to deal with crises." He had dealt with the Soviet Union and with the Middle East. But since then, he has turned his attention to disease, housing shortages, and democratic elections in developing countries around the world—"things I wasn't even aware of when I was president."

Two decades into his second career, Carter was awarded the Nobel Peace Prize for his humanitarian work. Whether you loved or hated him as president—or today resent or support his strongly held views about values and fundamentalism, he continues to have lasting impact on the lives of millions. After a crushing defeat, he created his new definition of success that, when you meet him, you're certain is much more meaningful to him than any that came before. He found a much better "job"—one that he's done for more than a quarter century and will do for the rest of his life.

"I would say that every created human being can be successful. Whether you are a retarded child or live in abject poverty or have any other defect in life, you can espouse the measurements of success in the eyes of God: justice, peace, humility, service, forgiveness, compassion, love. You don't have to be rich, powerful, famous, healthy, or intelligent to demonstrate those characteristics of life."

Carter's second career ushered in a new definition of what it means to be an American ex-president. George H.W. Bush, Sr. was also crushed by his loss at the end of his first term. But when he and his new friend, Bill Clinton, took unprecedented steps to join forces in Hurricane Katrina's wake in 2005 and the tsunami of 2004, both demonstrated renewed commitment to move on to new jobs on the international stage, rather than their old, highly successful roles as adversaries supporting their respective political parties. Both presidents had led relatively quiet lives for many years after their final terms before reengaging with issues in a highly visible way. But when they did, they applied the core value that never fades for enduringly successful people: integrity to meaning that makes a difference in their lives.

Even before leaving the White House, Clinton told us that he admired Carter's example more than any other and that he had assumed he would eventually take a similar path. Whether his high-profile, star-studded Clinton Global Initiative was selfless service or his own charismatic center stage leadership style bouncing back into high gear, it doesn't matter. If Clinton's colossal pledges from donors—

topping $2 billion for some 200 social projects—end up kick starting another 20 or 30 years of public service that genuinely means something to him, then he will have built enduring success, hand in hand with a legacy of lasting impact in his new career. Global leaders carry that burden if they want success to endure.

About a half dozen years after leaving office, George Bush, Sr., created and launched The George Bush Award for Excellence in Public Service, selecting people for the honor whose work reflected core values he shared with them, such as integrity to meaning and a courageous commitment to making a difference. Those he honored include former German Chancellor Helmut Kohl, former Soviet leader Mikhail Gorbachev, Democratic Senator Edward Kennedy, and evangelist Billy Graham. Bush lauded Graham, like the other three, for tireless devotion to deeply held beliefs that last.

Indeed, Graham's work has continued for more than a half century. He has been "an icon essential to a country in which, for two centuries now, religion has been not the opiate but the poetry of the people,"[4] notes *Time Magazine* when listing him among the *100 Most Important People of the (20th) Century*. "His sincerity, transparent and convincing, cannot be denied." As many U.S. presidents have learned, you "don't run for office among us by proclaiming your skepticism or by deprecating Billy Graham."

Although Builders keep their lives and careers on track by placing high value on personal meaning, individual interpretation and expression of "what matters" varies enormously. In the case of entrepreneur Richard Branson, what he wants to do is cut through the clutter to make an impression on certain types of customers so that he can "give them a better deal." What matters to spiritual leaders like Rabbi Singer of the World Jewish Congress and His Holiness the 14th the Dalai Lama Tenzin Gyatso isn't just selling their own brands of spirituality, as much as it is that they would like to bring peace and unity to the world to get people to buy into their own religions in a way that forms a bridge among people of all faiths.

Imagine Branson and the Dalai Lama in their own respective corners of the earth at the same moment in time. The head of state and spiritual leader of the Tibetan people is making his silent pilgrimage to prayer. Half a world away, it's a hot, sticky summer day in Oxfordshire. Sir Richard is cranking up the volume and sexual innuendo for a screaming crowd, while a celibate Lama chants cross-legged in his bright orange robes next to his lukewarm tea. Mark Thompson asked this "ordinary monk," as he calls himself, what passions he had not addressed in his life. He glanced down, fixing his gaze conspicuously below his navel, then looked up and with eyes twinkling, "But my life has been less complicated without it."

Like many spiritual leaders, when the Dalai Lama appears in New York's Central Park (and every other stop on his world tours), he draws standing-room-only crowds. His "gate" numbers would be the envy of any rock concert promoter, including Branson. What is important here is that, although Branson and the Dalai Lama have vastly different, even opposite ways of going about it, if you take away the high theatre and colorful wardrobe, at the core they are both populists. Here, their values overlap.

Each of them is pursuing an underdog, against-all-odds story—beating a path away from the big monopolies of fundamentalism. They both want to deliver what they think is a better way for regular people and the rest of the world. They believe that values like individual creative expression and happiness—for their own sake—provide meaning in our lives to which we should all aspire, no matter how nonintuitive, impractical, or dangerous that may seem.

As it turns out, all of the stories of enduringly successful people have some improbable quality to them. What helps successful people stay successful is their stubbornness about sticking with their own journey based on their own values, not a magic path followed precisely by everyone else. The lesson here is that you can't—or shouldn't—hijack someone else's value system. To do so would be a violation of integrity to what matters in your life. There is no more personal decision than to discover what meaning means to you. Only you can make that choice.

> *As it turns out, all of the stories of enduringly successful people have some improbable quality to them.*

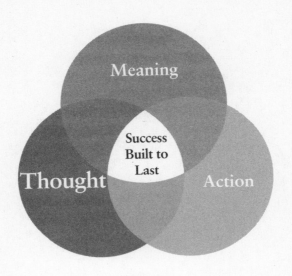

PART II

*ThoughtStyles—Extreme Makeovers
Start in Your Head*

About Thought ✳ Introducing ThoughtStyles ✳
How Extreme Makeovers start in your head ✳
About trusting your weaknesses ✳ Using your core
incompetencies to create success that lasts

---

*"Well, let's settle it. The first ThoughtStyle for success
that lasts is this: Success is not externally dependent."*

CHAPTER 5

The Silent Scream—Why It's So Damn Hard to Do What Matters

*Those who do not know how to weep with their wholeheart
don't know how to laugh either.*
—Golda Meir

*It's like the Wizard of Oz. We're looking for a wizard
seeking a heart, a brain, courage, and the wizard says you
already have these things. All you need to do is to use it.
When you believe in your great indomitable self,
then all things are possible.*
—Marva Collins

There are at least four good reasons (notice you always have good reasons) to feel sidetracked, intimidated, and diverted from building the life you want to create. Successful people told us that they've been given far fewer reasons to follow their dreams than reasons they should abandon them.

"Feels sometimes like you're outnumbered and outgunned from the start!" sighed Ogilvy and Mather CEO, Shelly Lazarus, one of the world's most powerful people in advertising. She insisted that if you talk with people anywhere in the world (she has operations in over 70 countries), you'll witness the same litany about their rocky path. Almost every successful person has a story of internal torment, whether you're from Beijing or Boston, Brussels or Bangalore.

Think of yourself as a "hero in your own miniseries," said Lazarus. (Of course, we tend to do this anyway!) Whether you let the forces working against you get you down, or you choose instead to move boldly ahead with your plans, there will be suffering involved either way. But it's worth the fight. "The good news is that when you finally go after what is meaningful to you," she insisted, "you have happier endings."

The Silent Scream

Happy endings come from listening to that little voice inside your head—some call it the whisper—about what matters to you. It is a voice that echoes through every cell in your body, straining to be heard like a *silent scream*. It's a nagging, often irritating "need" craving a response.

> *Happy endings come from listening to that little voice inside your head—some call it the whisper—about what matters to you.*

The tragedy for most people is that there is a gaggle of other voices trying to drown out the whisper. Whether it's the ranting of your own self-doubt or the concerns of loved ones and business partners, there are many forces vested in seeing you not change. These forces would be more comfortable if risky notions—like following your passion—were locked silent in the basement of your soul. Even when your dream is bound and gagged downstairs, you can still hear and feel that desperate, distant cry in the middle of the night. With loud, "rational" voices shouting upstairs, chances are slim that you'll pay attention to the whispering voice of your spirit. This gag order on your dream, left in place, will make you miserable. Builders plow ahead despite self-doubt, delusional bosses, desperate spouses, and outlaw in-laws who have high control needs. And, of course, there are always those incoming hostiles—media messages proclaiming that without consuming the right stuff, you cannot be successful or happy.

Four Good Reasons to Give Up Right Now, Before You Do Something Really Stupid

There are at least four traps that undermine your ability to respond to the silent scream. You might think that enduringly successful people don't have these problems. Builders claim to have had more than their share of each, and you'll likely find them all too familiar.

Trap #1: It's Not Considered a Worthy Career

Assertions that your ideas won't make a worthy career are often a screen to hide worries (legitimate or otherwise) over security and scarcity. Enduringly successful people say this issue rarely comes up until you announce plans to do something just for the love of it. "For goodness sake, you can't make money doing that," the voices nag. "What were you thinking?" cries another. Builders rise above the noise.

As a child, Tom loved war toys and outer space, and developed a passion for naval history as a teen. Poor eyesight frustrated his hopes to serve in the military. After getting a degree in English, Tom got practical. He started working as an insurance broker, and then joined a brokerage firm owned by his wife's grandfather. He ended up buying the firm. It was a "good living." To leave this lucrative small business to become a novelist would have been lunacy.

For around a dozen years, Tom heard that silent scream as he tinkered around the edges of his dream. He devoured military literature in the name of research. Still, the only writing credits he accumulated were a letter to the editor and a brief article on the MX missile.[1]

Almost two decades passed before a novel emerged. In his early forties, Thomas Leo Clancy Jr.'s first book, *The Hunt for Red October*, was published.[2] Literary reviewers to this day still say his writing isn't great, but his thrillers sell like hotcakes—as books, videogames, and motion pictures.

By his 50th birthday, he had a string of huge hits on the bestseller list and signed a book deal with Pearson Custom Publishing and Penguin Putnam, Inc. (both part of Pearson Education), which paid him $50 million for the world (English language only) rights for just two of his many books. He then signed another agreement ($25 million on this one) for a four-year book/multimedia deal. And Tom was just getting warmed up!

Granted, you won't run across a Tom Clancy every day of the week. But here's the deal: Enduringly successful people eventually answer the silent scream. Whether perceived by others as worthy or not—at some point in their journey, they embrace their dream for better or for worse. It is the only journey of lasting success.

Trap #2: Bright Shiny Objects for Our Driveways, Resumes, and Ring Fingers

If popular culture had its way, our lives would be dedicated to the relentless pursuit of things we are told we can't live without—as if it was actually true that things go better with Coke, $200 sneakers, cool clothes, and personality dialysis, plus a new, different, and better wife, husband, lover, friend, and coworker.

We want to impress colleagues and satisfy loved ones with achievements we think they'll envy. At the same time, we seek escape from the pain of envy ourselves. Craving acceptance, we pack our driveways, resumes, and ring fingers with what we call BSOs—*Bright Shiny Objects*—fancy cars, club memberships, designer clothing, advanced degrees, high-priced real estate, or anything else that's paraded as belonging to the lifestyles of the rich, smart, and famous.

This is not some high-minded, hypocritical pitch to abandon your material things or your education. (We're rather fond of our own, and we met plenty of Builders who love the things that they have.) Too many experts who claim to be antimaterialist have their own secret stash, or are trading up to bigger BSOs—like more fame, power, or spiritual elitism, to feed the ever-hungry ego monster.

For the most part, we didn't hear that anything was inherently bad about BSOs, but on the other hand, no Builder said that they expect these things to keep them happy.

DO WE HAVE OUR THINGS OR DO OUR THINGS HAVE US?

Although there may be nothing intrinsically wrong with having stuff, too many of us get lost on a treadmill of acquisition, chasing whatever we believe things will go better with. The trouble is, you can never get enough of what you don't really need to make you happy. No wonder folks become chronically depressed! As the Rolling Stones belted out, "I can't get no satisfaction." For satisfaction, you have to listen to what matters to you, not what is blaring from the mouths of friends, foes, and family.

It's ironic that if you become wealthier, for example, and your appetite for having nicer material things increases, there is an increasing risk that very little that you run across in the world is good enough. The more you're self-conscious of being judged by others for your higher standards of taste and material possessions, the world you may tolerate shrinks. Worse yet, the less of it you may actually enjoy. Instead of experiencing a greater diversity of pleasures with effortless ease, the stress and imagined obligation of showing up with style increases.

David Stern has had a front-row seat on the perils of superstardom and BSOs for 40 years. The commissioner of the National Basketball Association has a reputation for being tough—even controversial—on the job, but he's one of the most down-to-earth, engaging people when you meet him. He told us that the athletes "who love the game for the challenge," more than the "distracting goodies" that it can provide, seem not surprisingly to have better relationships, fewer problems, and "fun for the long haul," he said.

Stern heard his own silent scream four decades ago when he graduated from Columbia Law School and started doing outside legal work for the NBA. He loved it even though the future of the fledgling NBA was somewhat uncertain at the time. He was recruited to join full time as an employee "for a two-year stint," he said, to start the NBA's internal legal department in 1978. He was elected commissioner in 1984, the same year that basketball legend Michael Jordan turned professional. Stern engineered a turnaround of the near-bankrupt NBA back then to an enormously successful, swiftly growing global brand over two decades.

"The role when I first stepped in was crisis manager. It was lawsuits between owners and leagues, lawsuits between players and leagues, and really spending so much time focusing on collective bargaining and just getting through the day—worrying about merging clubs, not meeting pay-roll, how do we do it, and actually, drug scandals. Early on, we had players who were found to have used drugs and we dealt with the issue of being the first league where those revelations were made. And so we had to deal with that," he said. The NBA had no glamour or BSOs to sustain Stern's commitment in those difficult times. It was his loyalty to personal meaning—the silent scream—his passion that kept him going.

"In the old days, we were the opposite of Groucho Marx. We'd be happy to go to any club that would have us. And when you're struggling, that's the way you are."

You're better off when you remember to be grateful—when you never forget where you came from and what little you used to have, he said.

BSOs and the Afterlife

A simple way to look at whether BSOs own you—or whether you own them—is to ask yourself: Would you still want that stuff if people who mattered to you didn't care one way or the other? How about if they hated it? The idea here is to see whose BSO this is. Ultimately, no form of acquisition (having) or activity (doing) can lastingly deliver what we long for—the authentic experience of being fully alive.

> *Ultimately, no form of acquisition (having) or activity (doing) can lastingly deliver what we long for—the authentic experience of being fully alive.*

A popular exercise in leadership training is to have you write your eulogy. The problem here is participants tend to create a lofty list of things that sound impressive or heartwarming to the other people in the room—as if the exercise was a competition to be voted the most popular dead guy! (Move over, *American Idol*!) At your real funeral, your loved ones will spin a tale about you that makes them feel good. "If you want to know the truth," said networking king Keith Ferrazzi, author of *Never Eat Alone*, "go to the cocktail party afterwards and hear what that fellow was really all about."

Brazilian psychologist Tina de Souza recalled "I was talking to one client who said she hates to have someone touch her possessions. 'Oh, don't touch my car. Don't open my armoire, or don't do this or that because it's mine, it's mine, it's mine.' The poor woman was so anguished. I told her, 'Listen—imagine if right now you died. Okay? You're gone. Now think about your stuff, your beautiful dresses in your armoire. Probably right now, the people who love you, your family, or your neighbor, they are going through organizing your treasures. Who wants this ugly thing? Who wants that? Why did she marry him?'" Everything you left behind will be handled, misunderstood, and second guessed, she said. Under those circumstances, what is still important to you?

When you visualize your possessions and relationships from the perspective of being dead, hopefully, you'll find people and things that you actually do care about. This is kind of a brutal way to think about it, but it's interesting to see what still matters when you actually do this. Does any of it really mean anything? Don't assume that just because something is a thing, it shouldn't really matter. Take an open and honest inventory without pre-judging what should be good or bad. When you use your imagination to shuffle through your stuff and your relationships post mortem, you can gain some priceless insight into where to invest more or less of your time and energy.

Trap #3: The Seduction of Competence

From our earliest moments, most of us are told to make something of ourselves. But chances are that the people who tell you what you should make of yourself have no good idea of what to make of themselves. It's a mistake to make major choices about your career and your life based entirely on chasing a dream promoted by other people.

"Conventional wisdom has it that you should look to those who know you best," says Herminia Ibarra in *How to Stay Stuck in the Wrong Career*.[3] "Friends and family—with whom you share a long history—can offer insight into your true nature, and they have your best interests at heart; professionals add a dose of pragmatism, keep you grounded in the realities of the marketplace. But when it comes to reinventing ourselves, the people who know best are the ones most likely to hinder rather than help us. They may wish to be supportive, but they tend to reinforce—or even desperately try to preserve—the old identities we are trying to shed."

Beware of your natural tendency to rationalize what you should or ought to do as defined by other people. Humans are rationalization machines. One thing we often rationalize is working to become pretty good at a profession we don't particularly like.

The difference between pretty good and great is huge; it's the difference between a life that's half full and success built to last. Let's call it the *Seduction of Competence* (or the natural tendency we have to follow a False Profit.) If you're like most people, you are perfectly capable of developing adequate skills for a career chosen under social or economic pressures—usually self-imposed, but often as a result of being seduced into doing something politically correct to please others by giving them what they expect. Perhaps you chose as you did because it gave you status—or because it was something you thought would be a "safe" choice. There are no safe choices when it comes to lasting success unless the selection is based on real meaning.

Do you care more about being loved than being what you love? Do you feel you have to choose between the people who matter to you and doing the things that matter to you?

> *Do you care more about being loved than being what you love?*

JOY IN THIS WORLD IS ALWAYS IN SPITE OF SOMETHING

In his book *Talking to Ducks*, James A. Kitchens explains there are two major types of joy: internal joy and external joy. Internal joy comes from within, but external joy comes and goes with whatever is happening in our environment. It is extrinsic because it arises from the outside. When the circumstances change in one direction, joy comes. When fortune reverses, joy vanishes.

People who have found success that lasts pursue their goals because they matter to them, often despite popularity or recognition. Most people do it the opposite way: They do things despite what matters to them and because of their need for popularity or recognition.

Yvon Chouinard never seemed to worry much about political correctness. He started climbing mountains in 1953 when he was 14 years old and has been an outspoken environmentalist for decades. Climbers of that day climbed by placing single-use soft iron pitons—the only kind available—which were then left in the rock, defacing the environment. In 1957, he went to a junkyard and bought a used coal-fired forge, a 138-pound anvil, some tongs, and hammers, and started teaching himself how to blacksmith.[4] Chouinard, who became a world-class rock climber in his early twenties, made his first reusable pitons from an old harvester blade and tried them out on ascents of the Lost Arrow Chimney and the North Face of Sentinel Rock in Yosemite. The word spread, and soon friends had to have Chouinard's hardened steel reusable pitons. Before he knew it, he was in business—selling climbers the gear from the back of his car. He could forge two of his in an hour, and sold them for $1.50 each. He'd subsidize his income by collecting recyclable deposits on cans and bottles, thus serving the environment and allowing it to serve him.

As a staunch environmentalist, he claimed to be embarrassed about the idea of becoming a businessman. "I just really love the outdoors," Yvon said, "but I wasn't sure whether business was a worthy aspiration." Now nearly 70, this New Age outdoorsman claims that even today, it is as difficult to call himself a businessman as it is for "someone to admit to being an alcoholic or even a lawyer."

But he realized that he could use his company as a platform for many passions. In 1973, Chouinard led a group of surfers in Ventura, California, to found outdoor outfitter

Patagonia, Inc., a private company with current sales of over a quarter billion dollars. The firm's "mission statement is to use business to find solutions to the environmental crisis. I'm constantly pushing everyone in the company to realize that's why we are in business," he said. "That is the reason. We are not in the business to make a profit. We're not in the business to make a product. We're in the business to really change the way other companies operate." Chouinard, who is also author of *Let My People Go Surfing*, was not seduced away from his dream by his extreme aversion for business and the compromises that he and his community of green friends imagined it might require. He came to the conclusion that if you're going "to change the world and government," you can do that "inside out" by changing the way business is done.

WHEN HUMOR ISN'T A LAUGHING MATTER

"I started out as a dull municipal beat reporter writing about dull municipal meetings in the 1970s, many of which are still apparently going on," said humorist and bestselling author Dave Barry. "Then I became a dull writing coach vainly attempting to make dull business people become less dull. It was kind of a dull job. But everyone else thought it was a good idea. After all, it was a living," he said.

"I was already middle-aged and had a mortgage and family to support when the *Miami Herald* called." He had been moonlighting writing columns, and they invited him to take the plunge full time as a humor columnist. "It was scary [to leave a stable consulting job] but there was no other choice, in my view." For Barry, humor was an itch he had to scratch. It was a "relentless irritation. And believe me, comics aren't fun to be around when we're relentlessly irritated."

You may have noticed that some folks "hate happy people" just as much as they whine about unhappy people,

Barry said. When you find something that you love that matters to you, chasing that dream has a tendency to make you gush about it in ways that annoy the working stiffs around you.

In 1988, Barry won the Pulitzer Prize for Commentary and said that, not coincidentally, "I'm better at doing things that I'm good at, which tend to be things that I like doing." He says he has many friends and colleagues who have opted for following their passion—the silent scream—over the better judgment of well-meaning loved ones. "When they made the choice to do what they love, some started making more money and some didn't, but all are much better at what they do and they're having a blast."

IF YOU CRAVE ADULATION, GO WORK ON STAGE

"Some people do it for the attention," Barry said about his choice to become a columnist. "But that's a slippery slope. You never can predict what people will think of your work, and that changes day to day. If you crave adulation, then go work on stage. If you love to write, then write."

Someone who knows about the perils of public recognition is Sally Field, a director and actress who still commands popularity after four decades in television and film.

Having played silly roles as a beach babe, bad-boy girlfriend, and a flying nun, Field's early work never predicted her potential to be a serious actress or her Emmy- and Oscar-winning performances that followed.

"I haven't had an orthodox career, and I've wanted more than anything to have your respect," she told the Academy upon acceptance of her second Oscar. "The first time I didn't feel it, but this time I feel it, and I can't deny the fact that you like me, right now, you like me!"⁵ Most of us cringe when we think about this famously embarrassing admission. She has suffered lifelong parody for the remark.

You Can't Wait for a Standing Ovation to Validate What Matters to You

But you don't have to be in show business to have had that very same poignant worry about being loved in your heart. Now if you do—fess up (not in public, of course)—just admit it to yourself. We all know that not-so-silent scream demanding recognition. We may hate this part of us, yet our ego still clings to the craving, more or less. This egoistic need may never be entirely vanquished, but you must manage it if you want to enjoy lasting success. You can't wait for a standing ovation to validate what matters to you.

Rob Reiner played Michael "Meathead" Stivic in the classic Emmy Award-winning series *All in the Family*, and has directed several movies, including *When Harry Met Sally*. There is a classic scene in that 1989 film where Billy Crystal sits blandly at Katz's Deli with Meg Ryan, who fakes an orgasm to the stunned delight of those within earshot.

"I'll have what she's having!" a breathless diner exclaims, overhearing the performance. (Turns out the woman was Estelle Reiner, Rob's mother, and Billy Crystal is credited with the legendary wisecrack.)

"But isn't that what we all want out of life?" Reiner asked. We see someone else filled with extraordinary excitement—experiencing joy without relying on public acceptance or political correctness—wouldn't you want that in your life without faking it? "Well, I think that's what you want hopefully, to…feel that kind of freedom and that kind of happiness. We'd all like that."

Sally Field thinks she has one practical way to do that.

"The only thing you have power over is to get good at what you do. That's all there is; there ain't no more!" Field ranted to us about how much better off she is in her life when she's doing what she loves rather than "working on herself," sitting around worrying about what other people think about what she should be doing. You'll be hearing much more on how taking action beats navel gazing later in this book.

"It's the 'sitting and kvetching' that drives you nuts." If you do that, you're at risk of being seduced back into doing politically correct things rather than doing what matters to you. "And the way you become a leader, a role model, or any such, you know, high-falutin' terminology, is to have something to give back. The only way you have something to give back is to go do something; get off your rear end and go DO something! And that doesn't mean I'm going to go, you know, build housing for the underprivileged—that's good too, but go become a doctor, a lawyer, an Indian Chief. Go work your tail off and achieve something for yourself—some specific thing. Become excellent at something, at anything, you love."

"And if you say, I don't have anything I love, well then there's a real problem right there, and you have to sit down and say, 'Why don't I have anything that I love?' What in me has walked away from every inclination that I had, that I had found something, something that sparked me, something that was for me, and I didn't do it. You have to go back, you know, just recount every moment of your life, what was it, what was that one thing that I did that I loved?" said Field.

Many people wait for an epiphany—to be "hit by lightning" or hear an unambiguous answer delivered at the decibel level of a rock concert. It almost never goes down like this. The reality is that it usually takes years of hemming and hawing, or trial and tribulation, of trying and not quite getting it right, but feeling closer and closer, warmer and warmer, to the real thing. This is often a subtle connect-the-dots affair.

Sometimes, you'll have one moment that seems to catalyze everything into clarity, but that discovery is usually an outcome of trying a lot of stuff to see what works (also an idea explored in *Built to Last*). Eventually, it all makes sense after much hand wringing and experimentation, but not always at the beginning.

Trap #4: The "Tyranny of the OR"

One major source of guilt and confusion about the silent scream comes from the conundrum about whether to please you OR please others. Society counts on you for the latter. And you're afraid it may be too damn self-serving to do the former.

But Builders think differently about that: Does it get you excited AND help others at the same time? Does it serve you and serve others? For enduringly successful people, life is rarely a matter of either/or. What you hear from high achievers is that when you see your work as doing good and doing well, you stick with it through thick and thin.

Leaders of "visionary" organizations think in terms of the "Genius of the AND rather than the Tyranny of the OR."[6] For example, they don't see making money AND making a difference as a contradiction. That's also true for enduringly successful people. They don't believe that the choice is between serving a cause OR serving themselves. They choose both. Moreover, for Builders, the genius of the AND is not a fifty-fifty deal; it's a hundred-hundred deal. The passion that gets them up in the morning is just as much about what turns them on as it is about what it does for others. Enduringly successful people have concluded that their commitment to the service of others is also in their self-interest.

> Enduringly successful people have concluded that their commitment to the service of others is also in their self-interest.

When it comes to their goals, they're practical AND idealistic at the same time. They devote themselves to what they are trying to build over the long term AND focus on getting things done every day—and validation by the world is not their first concern.[7]

In fact, the genius of the AND is not just a matter of balancing the short term and long term—or accounting for your needs and those of outside stakeholders. It's all that and more. There are actually three legs on this stool, or rather, three circles, as you saw in Chapter 1, "From Great to *Lasting*—Redefining Success." It's a matter of getting meaning AND thought AND action all in alignment to get things done.

Note that serving others is not the same as pleasing others. Most of us feel the need to "get our ticket punched"—external validation that our mission has meaning—to rationalize that indeed, what we do matters. In the process of consciously or unconsciously pursuing being loved, we inevitably undermine the creation of what we love.

IF YOU HAVEN'T FOUND YOUR LOVER YET, KEEP LOOKING

"The only way to be truly satisfied is to do what you believe is great work," said Apple cofounder and CEO, Steve Jobs, in his now famous and intimate 2005 commencement speech at Stanford University.[8] "And the only way to do great work is to love what you do. If you haven't found it yet, keep looking. And that is as true for your work as it is for your lovers. As with all matters of the heart, you'll know when you find it. And, like any great relationship, it just gets better and better as the years roll on. So keep looking until you find it. Don't settle," he insisted.

Job's unwed mother was struggling and decided to put him up for adoption and better his opportunities before he was born. When she learned that the family that was about to adopt him didn't have college degrees, she panicked, refusing to sign the papers for months, until the new parents promised to give Steve access to a first-class education. To the working-class family, this was a challenging commitment.

"I had no idea what I wanted to do with my life and no idea how college was going to help me figure it out. And here I was spending all of the money my parents had saved their entire life. So I decided to drop out (after just six months) and trust that it would all work out okay. It was pretty scary at the time, but looking back, it was one of the best decisions I ever made," Jobs told the Stanford graduates.

"I didn't have a dorm room, so I slept on the floor in friends' rooms, I returned Coke bottles for the nickel deposits to buy food with, and I would walk the seven miles across town every Sunday night to get one good meal a week at the Hare Krishna temple. I loved it. And much of what I stumbled into by following my curiosity and intuition turned out to be priceless later on."

As a dropout, Jobs could take any "class" he wanted, and he was seduced by the beauty and grace of a novel (to him) art form: calligraphy. "None of this had even a hope of any practical application in my life," he thought. But it was that passion for beautiful type that came back to him ten years later when he was designing the Mac. Had he not taken that class, "personal computers might not have the wonderful typography that they do. Of course, it was impossible to connect the dots looking forward when I was in college. But it was very, very clear looking backwards ten years later."

When Steve Jobs and Steve Wozniak started Apple in the 1970s, they had a bold goal to put a computer in every home. The two Steves accurately predicted the future, except it was not their company that shipped all those PCs. Apple is hotter and hipper and growing faster today than it has in years, but it still has a relatively small market share after more than 30 years in business.

What may be more important is that Job's early vision to create a beautiful and useful electronic canvas has defined computing for all time. This lasting impact on history will outlive the man and his company. Living your passion despite all odds may not make you the biggest or the richest player, but is this what matters? Try to imagine a world without Apple and Pixar, and you realize what it means to bring creativity and beauty to a technology that had neither before these companies provided both. Builders say a legacy like this is what makes life worth living.

"Your time is limited, so don't waste it living someone else's life," Jobs insisted. "Don't be trapped by dogma—which is living with the results of other people's thinking. Don't let the noise of others' opinions drown out your own inner voice—and most important—have the courage to follow your heart and intuition. They somehow already know what you truly want to become. Everything else is secondary."

> *"Your time is limited, so don't waste it living someone else's life."*

The lesson we take from highly accomplished people is to be mindful about what you wish for, but don't let that stop you on your path to redefining success. Doing things despite, not because of, the political correctness of the path—whether it's a small step in your life or a giant one in your career—is the price of admission to almost every enduring life of lasting impact.

CHAPTER 6

The Cause Has Charisma—
You Don't Have to Be Charismatic
to Be Successful

You give birth to that on which you fix your mind.
—Antoine de Saint-Exupery

She paced nervously in a seedy alley between 16th and 17th Street in San Francisco, trying to "do enough jobs" to pay her pusher, when an outrageous thought hit her around 3 A.M. "I'm out walking the streets, addicted, homeless, sleeping in the gutter, and someday I am going to be in a place where I'm supposed to be telling people about this horror. I am supposed to change things," Norma Hotaling remembered.

"Of course, the next thought I had completely killed that hopeful idea. *You're just a whore on dope—and that is all you'll ever be.*" Norma grimaced and sighed, running her hand through her hair. She has a plate, wires, and screws in her skull to patch the beating she took when she dumped a pimp. Every morning, she would find her way to a dingy hotel where dealers and addicts hung out. "It would be a nightmare when I got there—the smell—and noise—of homeless people wired and hallucinating. You'd never know what you were walking into, particularly if you were short of money. Sometimes, I'd come in without an 'outfit' (a needle) and couldn't find a way to clean it when

I borrowed one." It would be several more dangerous years of struggle to get off, then on, then off heroin and cocaine, before she finally got herself locked in a jail cell again to detox one last time.

When Norma Hotaling got out of "the business," her pals tried to coerce her back onto the street, and city officials called her unqualified when she announced she would open The Sage Project, a center to help other women get out of the business and into a life. Today, Hotaling squeezes her dream into several tiny cubicles packed between unpainted walls behind a locked iron gate in San Francisco's Mission District. As an ex-prostitute, ex-felon, and ex-heroine addict, she still feels dreadfully inadequate when she hears herself being called a leader. But after 30 years "out there in the gutter watching friends die, there are too damn many other girls to save" to allow her lack of a social worker's pedigree to get in the way of getting women off the street. In reality, it is the pedigree of her personal experience of their plight that enables her to lead their escape from the vicious cycle of drugs and prostitution.

It didn't help her to know that while she struggled with her own recovery from abuse, many of the people she approached for support didn't think she was up to the task she had chosen. "No one is lower on the social totem pole than someone who has been an addict and whore," she said.

Actually, when she wanted help badly enough to passionately seek it out, "incredible people came forward to help." She connected with people who lived their lives with purpose and that, in turn, encouraged her to live her life with purpose. With the passage of time, the team of people supporting her work just grew and grew.

Due to hardship, genes, or both, many of the Builders we interviewed lacked the kind of confidence you might expect in a leader. Many were tentative, even nervous, introverts. But when they talk about what really matters to them, it's like watching shy, mild-mannered Clark Kent step into a phone booth and, a moment later, out leaps a super hero. Despite the way Norma Hotaling feels about herself at any given moment, her cause has the charisma she needs to keep her going through hard times, help her magnetize and motivate a strong support community, and unlock barriers such as low self-esteem and limited knowledge in an area.

"It came down to this," Hotaling insisted, eyes welling. "I will do this and make a difference, or I'll commit suicide. It's just that simple and just that hard." What could the rest of us accomplish with a fraction of that clarity?

"I'm extremely vulnerable and sensitive and (yet) here I am having to spill my guts, telling such a private story over and over again in public. I've done this work for two decades and it's very difficult," she said. "Every time I speak, there are unfeeling people out there who hate what I represent. Leadership is almost like being a martyr, if you let it be. So for a while, I thought I'd cope by keeping my new personal life separate from my new 'job' as a leader. That was a big mistake," Hotaling claimed.

"You can't disconnect what matters to you from your life. That was unhealthy and impossible for me. That's like prostitution again—in order to survive being raped for pay, you have to create a charge box for your separate body parts: my lips, my breasts, my vagina. But these are not separate parts of me, just as the meaning of my work cannot be separated from my life," she said.

"In order for you to do what matters in a way that you are healthy, you can't pretend or deaden out like a machine—to steel yourself doesn't work. You have to feel everything and use it. My story is not my job; my story is me—even when it hurts me to have to say it again. My cause is my life. It helps now to be more frank about the horror than I was five years ago when I was politically correct. I cry a lot more now and that helps."

> *"In order for you to do what matters in a way that you are healthy, you can't pretend or deaden out like a machine—to steel yourself doesn't work. You have to feel everything and use it."*

Hotaling was invited to Korea to meet with the leadership of nonprofit and government agencies after a three-year collaboration inspired by Sage's work resulted in new legislation. "I heard about a group of survivors—women who were actually willing to speak out about their plight despite the stigma." After struggling with logistics, Hotaling finally caught up with a group of 15 courageous women. "I travel alone around the world," she said. "But when I arrived, they leapt up—applauding and crying. We wept together. They said they were carrying on Sage's legacy half a world away. I wasn't alone anymore. I'm always working for and with my sisters."

That's what gets her up in the morning. Even when her emotions are descending into darkness, the light of her conviction reassures her that what she is building is bigger than she is. Fretting about whether or not she's up to the task gets overshadowed by the urgency of the need. It's something that must be done with or without her; it lives in her gut, and it would make her heart ache if she were not a part of it.

Now the world seems to be getting her message. Among many honors, Hotaling won a "Use Your Life" award from Oprah Winfrey, who applauded the courageous work of Sage that has saved hundreds of young women and runaways from crime, drugs, prostitution, and death.

"My 'spiritual advisory board' are the women who died," Hotaling said. "When I was scared and hopeless, I'd remember my sisters who had come before me and given their lives to understand what's needed."

The Courage to Move Forward

Many Builders will tell you that breaking away from the boundaries set in their own minds—despite the realities of their tortured past—was one of their most difficult, necessary, and rewarding achievements.

"De-colonizing your mind is the first step," said Roberta Jamieson, who became chief of the Six Nations of the Grand River, where she grew up. On her way to college, Jamieson was so appalled by the treatment of indigenous people that she dumped her premed ambitions to instead become the first aboriginal woman in Canada to earn a law degree. She also became one of the first attorneys in Canada to evangelize arbitration over litigation, based on the long history of peaceful dispute resolution known so well in her tribal community. Today, she is CEO of the National Aboriginal Achievement Foundation in Toronto.

"You must release yourself from the repression of your mind," she noted. "You are no longer a prisoner. You are not that person. You are a part of a long and great history. You are entitled to make decisions. You have gifts to share that belong to your people. It is your responsibility to share your talents with others. Throw off the shackles that keep you down—stop tearing at yourself and others because you don't feel good about yourself," Jamieson demanded.

"When you come into this world, you were given instructions—sort of a toolkit of your talents and special gifts that you are given. Your life's task is to put those tools to use for the seventh generation. How much purpose and power would you have if you knew your choices would impact your community and country for seven generations?" When Jamieson was asked to become chief, she turned it down twice. She finally accepted the job when it became clear to her that she uniquely contributed to what her people needed. Even so, at the end of her term, she went back to her day job. "The point was to serve when the service demanded it. I'm not the kind of person who wants to be the boss for its own sake."

Like Norma Hotaling, Jamieson was called to leadership because the cause itself had charisma. The same was true for scientist Dr. Francine "Penny" Patterson. She has never quite gotten comfortable with the idea of "leading" an organization, so she simply never looks at it this way.

As a girl, Penny would sneak lizards and snakes into her bedroom, watching them for hours and days, captivated by what the little critters might be thinking. "That was all it took to just completely mesmerize me," she said, her eyes shining. When she had the opportunity to care for a baby gorilla during graduate school at Stanford, she was thrilled.

"I couldn't believe my luck. I couldn't sleep the night before. I was nervous and excited about meeting what I considered the ultimate animal." She had no idea at the time that this temporary assignment would morph into the next 30 years of her life.

What nobody had counted on was that Patterson would, like a modern day Dr. Doolittle, boldly attempt to teach the gorilla sign language. The scientific community came unglued.

"There were conferences held that were designed to demonstrate that we were frauds," she sighed. "There were academicians and philosophers who decided that this was an impossible proposition, so something had to be wrong with it." Teaching an animal to have a human conversation was, needless to say, "Controversial—it changed the world view in a way that is uncomfortable for a lot of people." The attacks on her credibility were relentless.

"I think it is a blessing that I can dismiss those things so that I can focus on the positive and keep going. That's not true for all of my colleagues, some of whom can remember all criticism chapter and verse." But the stakes were too high, in Patterson's mind, to be seduced into the paralysis of a victim. "It could be a constant barrage that would actually drive you to depression—you could have just given up."

But she didn't. For more than three decades now, her passion has put this statuesque blond in a steel cage face-to-face with Koko, a great ape that has grown up to be a 300-pound hairy scholar that does math, paints high-priced masterpieces, "and is able to reveal her thoughts and feelings through the use of 1,000 gestural words."[1] You might remember the now famous cover of *National Geographic* showing a huge gorilla cradling a tiny kitten. That was Koko. She has transformed the world's perception of what a wild animal can be.

Having to spend 24/7 with Koko has been a lifelong pleasure for Patterson. Asking humans for support—well—that's been another thing entirely.

"I get hives when I have to do these meetings; psychologically, I am just totally a basket case—I have to ask very wealthy, very important people to support this cause. I have to convince them about what is at stake. I have to go one-on-one and it scares me."

The only thing that gets her through the queasiness is that she believes her cause has moral authority even when she feels she doesn't. Patterson hates to ask for money—she can barely stop trembling enough to dial the telephone number. Her voice quivers. But when she gets on the line with a potential sponsor, her heart bursts with charismatic energy:

"It's one minute before midnight, and then we lose them," she pleaded. "When the clock strikes 12, our closest cousin to humanity—the gorilla—will be dead and gone forever." Today, celebrities like Peter Gabriel, Sting, and Robin Williams make the job a bit easier.

When the Cause Has Charisma, Shrinking Violets Bloom in Public

The concept of the charismatic leader has been getting bad press lately. The critics may be missing the point. Whether or not you're shy, humble, outgoing, or assertive is not really the issue. Your personality is not what determines enduring success; it's what you do with your personality that counts. Whether you have too big or too small of an ego might create all sorts of problems, and we don't want to let you off the hook for bad behavior. We found that the personalities of Builders come in all sizes. They have all sorts of psychological issues that are better left for description by Dr. Phil.

> *Your personality is not what determines enduring success; it's what you do with your personality that counts.*

Some are painfully shy and others seem aggressively in-your-face—it just depends on whether or not you happen to care about what they care about. If you happen to be interested, they're interesting people. If you're not, some seem obnoxious.

The essential difference with Builders is that they've found something to do that matters to them and are therefore so passionately engaged, they rise above the personality baggage that would otherwise hold them down. Whatever they are doing has so much meaning to them that the cause itself provides charisma and they plug into it as if it was electrical current.

Enduringly successful people—whether they're shrinking violets or swashbuckling entrepreneurs—serve the cause, and it also serves them. It recruits them and they are lifted up by its power. When that happens for you, a bigger, more engaging version of "you" shows up.

Taiwanese-born engineer, Jen-Hsun Huang, founder and CEO of multibillion-dollar videochip maker, Nvidia, has always been ambitious, but a self-described introvert—until he steps up in front of the computer screen to show you what his team is working on. When he does that, it's as if he were kneeling before an altar—a shrine to his life's work. The deep reverence he has for the beauty and grace of what they build is visceral, if not a little odd, to non-techies. His awe for the cause is, in effect, the shrine. His excitement for the mission makes him seem—well—charismatic.

Although soft-spoken Huang maintains he would rather "be home playing with the kids or sitting quietly drinking a glass of wine with my wife," he no longer shows as strong an urge to run and hide, because he's talking about his favorite topic. When you put together deep knowledge about a subject that intensely matters to you, charisma happens. You gain courage to share your passion, and when you do that, folks follow. According to Peter Drucker, this makes you a leader.

Making Your Passion Take Flight

This is exactly what happened to Herb Kelleher, founder of Southwest Airlines. It's not that he wasn't already a fun engaging guy, but that he unexpectedly found a cause that changed an obscure lawyer's career into one that transformed an industry. Kelleher was called in as an outside attorney on an assignment to help an entrepreneur start an airline, and the next thing he knew, he had become a co-founder.

What hit him so unexpectedly was a populist passion to cure a perceived injustice—it was simply too expensive for the majority of Americans to fly. Perhaps this might not seem like a moral obligation, but for Kelleher, it felt that way. He was willing to sacrifice a lot to do something about it. He summoned the courage to go from being a capable lawyer with a reputable practice to being an unemployed entrepreneur willing to help others join him deeply in debt, in the name of the cause.

As is often the case when Builders are gripped by the power of what matters to them, Kelleher went from being a pretty good lawyer to an extraordinary leader. He had no idea his passion would help him become one of the most admired CEOs of all time, managing with a wit and self-deprecating humor still rarely seen in a corporate board-room. Nor did he realize his airline would achieve the longest-running history of profitability in an industry known more for bankruptcy than customer service.

What is often forgotten, and you need to know, is that the good-natured Kelleher had to withstand the siege of seemingly endless litigation from competitors just to get his dream off the ground. The day after Southwest's applica-tion was approved by the regulators, Braniff Airways[2] sued and Southwest lost the lawsuit. Then, Southwest lost again on appeal. Kelleher pleaded with his Board to keep trying and battled his way to the Texas Supreme Court, where he finally prevailed. It took Kelleher five turbulent years to get from the now-famous business-plan-on-a-paper-napkin to Southwest's first flight.

Imagine yourself bailing out of your nice, safe, well-respected professional job to become the subject of ridicule and litigation by the industry you want to reinvent, and then bleeding red ink for years to accomplish the goal. It happens all the time to pioneers. Kelleher was sustained by his passion for justice—the very reason he had become a lawyer in the first place—as he argued tirelessly not to achieve success, as traditionally defined as power, fame, and riches, but rather to serve a cause that mattered. It was his belief that the cause had charisma, he insists, that made his zealous, "unprecedented, irrational behavior possible." Braniff Airways has long since been out of business. On the other hand, Southwest is flying high, and the value segment of air travel has been forever redefined in ways that are catching on all over the world.

What If Your Dream Never Becomes Popular?

Popularity was never high on the list for Nadine Strossen. "I'm a lawyer, and I think that the law is a wonderful profession," said Dr. Strossen, a law professor at New York University. "But if you look at surveys of attitudes of lawyers, especially young lawyers, you see enormous unhappiness, malaise, and lack of excitement at best; real alienation and frustration at worst—whether you're talking about powerful partners at established Wall Street firms or solo practitioners," she said.

"The one exception I see is any lawyer in the profession who is somehow involved in using the law degree to advance his or her own conception of justice." Strossen's team has "this passionate commitment toward justice. We may have different conceptions of what that is, but we believe in it and therefore derive great joy from using our professional skills to advance it. It's fun as well as being good work in both senses of the word," she said.

"Isn't that why we're here?" shrugged Strossen, who graduated from Harvard Law School, brimming with hope that her own brand of populist justice could make a difference. "If it's worth doing, then for heaven's sake, treat it as if it's worth doing!" Leadership begins with you as an individual and your ability to improve your performance—to develop your expertise and excellence.[3]

If there was an attorney you might expect to be angry or unhappy, it would be Strossen. She volunteers to work for free as president of the American Civil Liberties Union (ACLU). It's hard to imagine an organization more under fire from all sides of the political spectrum.

"Clearly, I had to develop a tolerance for unfair criticism, and I found that amazingly easy," she claimed, "Perhaps because it is an organization that is being

> *"If it's worth doing, then for heaven's sake, treat it as if it's worth doing!"*

attacked rather than me as an individual." But she admits she is also assailed as an individual, too.

Strossen says she doesn't have "a thick skin in the sense that I am not insensitive and not open to see if there is at least a kernel of truth in criticism—something constructive that I can learn from it, as an individual or as the leader of my organization. But I do not let it incapacitate me in any way. I see the contrast, for example, with some of the younger employees in the ACLU or some of the less experienced ones who are shocked and really find it personally debilitating, and I have to give them pep talks to bring them along."

Strossen, who says she would "be willing to pay [the ACLU] to do this job," confidently reassured her troops. "Don't take it personally. And you can even see it as a compliment. People wouldn't see you as such a lightning rod, such a target, unless they saw that you were making headway on your agenda and their agenda is a very different one," she insisted.

"In some ways, I can say what Ronald Reagan once famously said about a criticism the ACLU had made of one of his policies." Strossen quoted the president: "He said, 'I hear the ACLU has criticized me. I [Reagan] wear that criticism like a badge of honor.' And I would say, well, when his [Reagan's] attorney general denounced us [the ACLU] as the criminal's lobby, I wore that as a badge of honor. You have to be an optimist in my line of work—or an idealist—or you could never carry forward. But the wonderful and exciting thing is the empowerment that one feels. The harder you work, the more energized you are by the justice of the cause and the opportunity to really make a difference in the lives of real people," Strossen said.

"My concept of leadership is not necessarily having a title, but exercising a certain kind of behavior. I use the term [leadership] more to describe what you do, rather than what position you happen to occupy. In other words, there are people who have prestigious titles—including a lot of elected officials—that to me are quintessential followers rather than leaders. They follow the shifting tides of public opinion and adjust their positions on the issue accordingly.

"So, my model always goes back to John F. Kennedy's *Profiles in Courage*—people who had the courage of their convictions through thick and thin. I think just about every character or historical figure in that book, at some point or another, was, in fact, voted out of office or denied office precisely because of that quality, which in my view made that person a leader whether or not he continued to be president or in the Senate."

Builders cling to a personal commitment that's so compelling to them—something so important to them that they would actually do it for free—that they must do it despite popularity, not because of it, the way Nadine Strossen does.

Trust Your Passion Enough to Become an Expert at It

Condoleezza Rice, like Strossen, lives her life in the crosshairs of public opinion and long ago found herself attracted to issues that moved her so much that she could not avoid them. When you meet both women, it's clear that their secret to survival and success has always been to go deep—to learn everything they possibly could about anything they deeply cared about.

Life takes "passion, determination, and skill," Rice cautioned. You can't skip any of those three and expect to enjoy success built to last.

Neither Rice nor Strossen picked career paths that would make them piles of money, but instead chose another kind of wealth and power: knowledge. If you should be greedy about anything, it should be about acquiring "intellectual capital" for your dream.

> Life takes "passion, determination, and skill," Rice cautioned. You can't skip any of those three and expect to enjoy success built to last.

When you have "earned" knowledge, as Professor Rice told students during her time at Stanford, you have an ethical responsibility to "invest" that capital—those skills—on making a difference in business or public service.

You could argue that Strossen and Rice have always been bordering on the obsessive—both are over-the-top overachievers who have worshipped their cause as it has drawn them to have extraordinary impact on the world.

Rice never thought it could be done any other way. She grew up in Birmingham, Alabama, when the Klu Klux Klan was still in business. When she was eight, a fellow schoolmate, Denise McNair, died in an explosion when white supremacists attacked a neighborhood Baptist church. Rice's parents, her father a minister at Westminster Presbyterian Church and her mother a music teacher, had the resources to insulate her from some of the discrimination she would have faced with lesser means. But Rice says she always assumed that she had to be better prepared as a woman and a minority—to go "twice as deep" to get ahead. Being superficial or taking her passions lightly were never options.

As a child, she was a competitive figure skater and played the flute, violin, and the piano (her favorite). Her mother decided to name her daughter based on an affectionate Italian expression in music composition, *Con Dolce* or *Con Dolcezza*, which means to play "with sweetness."

Today, her adversaries in international politics would think that ironic for one of the toughest, most powerful women in the world.

At 15, when her classmates back in Birmingham were finishing up their summer vacations after their freshman year in high school, ambitious Condi was already starting college as a music major at the University of Denver. She soon discovered that she was "good, but not good enough to be great at it," she said. Rice had wanted to be a virtuoso, not end up as a music teacher helping "13-year-olds murder Beethoven," she told ABC News. So at 16, the college sophomore went in search of a new major, and the world would never be the same.

It was a time when the Cold War with the Soviet Union cut planet Earth precariously in two. Here comes this brilliant black teenage girl from the Deep South who knew something about a divided world. Whether it was the gulf between her precocious genius and intellects of her peers, the extraordinary poise she exhibited at a relatively tender age compared with older college students, or the issues of color or class back home, Rice knew how wide the chasms were to cross in this nation and this world. She found that an irresistible challenge. She wasn't welcome in a hat shop in Birmingham, but she could become president of the United States. It was no surprise she decided to train for politics.

Rice happened upon one of the most central inspiring figures in her life when she attended the class of former Czech diplomat, Josef Korbel, who was talking about Stalinist Russia. (Korbel was father to another rising star in government, Madeleine Albright, who became President Clinton's Secretary of State.) Rice was captivated and dove headfirst into political science and international diplomacy. After getting her master's degree from the University of Notre Dame and her Ph.D. from the University of Denver, she became an assistant professor at Stanford when she was in her twenties.

Word of young, wiry Condi Rice's extraordinary talent for American and Russian politics got around. Rice's expertise—her passion for going deep—gave her more authority. President George H. W. Bush selected Rice to advise him on Soviet affairs in 1989, and soon she became his chief advisor for the summit meetings with Mikhail Gorbachev as the Soviet Union neared its collapse. According to journalist Steve Kettmann, Bush proudly introduced her to Gorbachev, "This is Condoleezza Rice. She tells me everything I know about the Soviet Union."[4]

Is Condi Rice an admirable public servant and/or a conservative hawk? Is Nadine Strossen an admirable public servant and/or a radical liberal? There are armies of people on either side of those positions. There are some who are uncomfortable seeing both women in the same book, let alone the same sentence. Loved or hated, Rice and Strossen draw enormous power and energy from their respective causes—demanding deep knowledge and commitment from themselves and their teams. That personal connection to meaning has substantially contributed to their ability to have high impact in their careers for a very long time.

Whatever You Are, Be a Great One

One of the best ways to unleash the charisma that Builders feel for a cause, calling, career, or other major objective, is to see whether or not they're really willing to immerse themselves in it. Opportunity comes from expertise, not just luck, talent, and passion. If you find it impossibly tedious to become an expert about what you think matters to you, then you're not chasing a dream, you're just daydreaming. You can't claim the buried treasure if you aren't willing to dig for it.

That is not to say that it's easy, or that you won't suffer frequently. But if you find you can't or won't persist in learning more and more about it, then it's going to be very tough to hang on when inevitable obstacles get thrown in your way. This isn't earth-shattering news. We heard this from everyone—being your best at what you do is essential to success built to last.

Former biotechnology entrepreneur, Ed Penhoet, now head of one of the world's largest foundations, thinks that your willingness to become great at what you do—for its own sake—is a key to success. After all, if you find it's impossible to go deep, then you've found out something valuable, too—you shouldn't be doing it, he said.

"I'm a big believer in fortune cookies," Penhoet grinned. "When I was a professor at Berkeley, I once got one that said, 'Whatever you are, be a good one.' And to me that's the only business advice I can give anybody. When you are good at one thing, doors open up in front of you. People want to work with you, so people provide opportunities to you. You don't have to go looking for them. Usually, they come to find you," he said.

"Success is always built on doing well the job that's in front of you today, not being resentful that you don't have a CEO job yet," Penhoet said. "In fact, it's an amazing phenomenon. I see it in MBAs in particular. They all think because they have an MBA, they ought to be at least a senior vice president (by) the next week. But what they need to do is prove that they can actually do something well," Penhoet insisted.

"In my own life, I found that people who are always worried about the next move in the chess game of their life never quite get at that move. Don't think that way because, if you're always worrying about the next step, it will compromise your ability to do your current job well," Penhoet said.

> *I found that people who are always worried about the next move in the chess game of their life never quite get at that move.*

People get to know you as the person who does a good job or the one who does a bad job, Penhoet said. You won't "be remembered as having done *that* job badly—you'll be remembered as a person who does a bad job," he said.

When Builders found that striving for excellence is unreachable, joyless, or the kind of misery you find in a Stephen King horror movie, they saw it as a message to move onto something else. For the cause to have charisma, it must reach into your heart in a personal way to unlock all you have to give.

It Starts with You, But Ultimately, It's Not About You

In fact, after you're focused on what you believe needs to be done, you will have more energy to persist despite inevitable resistance from other people. School teacher Marva Collins runs into a wall almost every time she introduces her new program to educators. "I still have a great challenge today when I go into schools to put in my methodology or to work with a school; many of the teachers will not speak to me, or have a very negative attitude. But the attitude isn't about me; it's that they do not believe in their excellence as much as I see that they're excellent," she said.

"So I have learned to look at that in a different perspective—because I think if you somehow concentrate on the wrongs that have been done to you (the criticism), you will never evolve. And if you do not evolve, you're not growing," she insisted. She says that the pushback that she gets often isn't as much about her as it is about how those people feel about themselves. The problem is that their cause doesn't have charisma for them.

"I was ridiculed by the other teachers," Collins lamented her early days as a school teacher. "Even the principal said to me, 'Your problem is you cannot forget that these are not your children. They come from fettered homes, antecedent homes; you cannot have the same expectations for them.'"

Collins grew up in poverty in Alabama with the hope that she would get an education. She ended up influencing public education in Chicago. Collins has been so admired for the results she achieved with "hopeless" students that Presidents Reagan and Bush, Sr., asked her to serve as Secretary of Education (but she chose instead to stick with her passion in the classroom). Today, her methods are a model in dozens of communities across America.

"When you're swimming upstream in a nation where the average conversation is 'what's wrong with the children,' and I am telling them what's right with the children—well, that's not a conversation that wants to be heard." So after 14 years of battling, of "seeing such lowered expectations for our children," Marva Collins started her own school, funding it out of her own pocketbook.

The World Would Be a Darker Place Without You

Collins believes she can change the world by helping children believe that the world would be a darker place without each of them. "There's a line in *Moby Dick* that says, 'in the slippery world, we all need something to hold on to,' and we aren't giving our children something to hold on to. You can't hold on to computers and computer games, and designer clothing, and how lovely you are, how handsome you are. You have to hold on to that one person, that wherever you go, there you are. And that's the self that we each are." That is the self that hears the whisper about what matters to you and tells you which cause or calling will have the charisma to light up your life.

When you can come to the point where you accept yourself for who you are—"warts and all"—and you can embrace what you love, for better or for worse, you have a better chance of finding lasting success.

"The first question I ask teachers that I train is, 'What's wrong with the children?' I get a litany of answers," she noted. "My next question is, 'What's wrong with the parents?' The answers are infinite. The third question is, 'What's wrong with you as a teacher?' And, of course, I get complete silence. We have to begin with what's wrong with us that (puts us in a position where we feel) we can't help this child? If you begin with *these* children, *those* parents, *that* principal; they don't know this, they don't know that. If we begin with all those negatives, we will never get to where children can go." Collins believes that you must ask "not just what your cause can do for you," but what you can do for your cause. When you can "feed the cause and it also feeds you," then you will make a difference and develop your confidence.

Self-Esteem Is Highly Overrated

Maybe you thought you would wait to tackle your persistent passion when you had more self-confidence. Well, do the work and accomplish something and, *voila*, you'll gain that confidence. Self-esteem is highly overrated.[5] There are criminals who rate highly on confidence tests and saints who score pretty low. Marva Collins wants parents, kids, and teachers to know that they are capable of excellence. She does not advise them to wait for self-confidence, nor does she want them to believe success is an entitlement. It's not about whether you have high or low self-esteem; it's about the quality of your effort.

When a student turns in a paper far below the mark, Collins doesn't judge it as bad or give him or her a failing grade and move on. Instead, she asks, "Do you want this to be a paper worth 50 cents, $50, or $5 million?" She points out how they are capable of all three outcomes and could go about achieving any of them.

"We teach children that someone lived happily ever after," she said, and that they can take shortcuts or take the easy way out. That just cheats them from the opportunity to build the kind of skills that will give them more confidence. "We don't teach them how to get through bad times—that's why these kids are killing each other and blowing up schools. We must teach children that there are bad times and how to get through the bad times and that life is not a happily-ever-after endeavor."

You've got to fail on the path to success, Collins said. This can be a tired cliché, of course, but it is also a fact. As you will see in the next chapter, Builders believe adversity provides the opportunity to get better at what you do—to go from average to extraordinary—and to test what you really care about. "You're going to make mistakes" if you try anything that is worth doing, Collins said. What is important is to "remove labels" that hold you back from realizing you "can be a champion."

Don't wait for a day when you feel good about yourself to get started. Builders insist that self-esteem comes from trying and failing, trying and failing, then succeeding with small wins and doing the work a little better each time. That tenacity comes when a cause has the charisma to pull you through hard times and unleash your passion for going deep in ways that drive you to do more than you might have ever imagined you could do.

> *Builders insist that self-esteem comes from trying and failing, trying and failing, then succeeding with small wins and doing the work a little better each time.*

CHAPTER 7

The *Tripping* Point—Always Make New Mistakes

Experience is a hard teacher. She gives the test first, the lesson afterwards.
—Dick Enberg[1]

Gain is the edge of loss; loss is the heart of gain. Having many difficulties perfects the being; having no difficulties ruins the being."
—Lao Tzu

The fellow asked the bearded sage he met on the path, "Which way is success?" The monk said nothing and gestured down the path. The seeker was elated by the prospect that success was so close and so easy, and rushed ahead.

Suddenly, there comes the sound of *splat*. In a little while, the seeker, now tattered and stunned, limps back, assuming he must have taken a wrong turn. He repeats his question to the guru, who again points silently in the same direction.

The seeker nods, turns, and heads back in the same direction as before. This time, the sound of *splat* is deafening. When the seeker crawls back, he is bloody, broken, and angry. Screaming at the monk, he demands to know why he was sent off in the direction of disaster. "No more pointing. Talk!"

Only then does the guru speak. "Success is that way," he said. "Just a little past splat."

It's human nature to love hearing about mishaps—as long as they belong to other people, particularly successful people. We never met a soul who didn't have a pile of embarrassments or stunning defeats in their portfolio. Many highly accomplished people described themselves as so proficient at making mistakes that, if you didn't know better, you might think they were losers. If there was just one thing that every enduringly successful person we met had in common, it is that they are all really great at failure.

Life Is Short, But Some Days Are Really Long

Humor makes it a whole lot easier for you to accept who you are and what happens to you. But if you can laugh at adversity and enjoy this kind of rough-and-tumble learning in your personal life and work, you're a rare bird. Not many enduringly successful people find their own foolish foibles funny. Builders may seem to be able to grin and bear it under the most difficult of circumstance, but they suffer like the rest of us. Although we might put them high on a pedestal, crediting them with superhuman attributes, it's usually just so we don't feel pressured to aspire to their heights. We tear them down just as quickly as icons when they fail to live up to hyped-up expectations.

Many Builders face lifelong adversity, phobias, or flaws that they never overcome—but they do find a way to manage them. They refuse to let their goals and dreams be held ransom by their feelings in that awful moment when everything has gone wrong.

"The hurt of it all is there and to pretend that it's not isn't healthy," said physician Martha Reitman, talking about her own journey as a Builder. "When you get a body blow, you're going to go into shock for awhile, and then all the gradual stages of mourning occur—from hurt, to guilt, to anger, to recovery. Acknowledging that is critically important if you're going to deal with it. That's when you can start to get solace from the doing. You can rebuild, you can make use of this—and that's very affirming. It's a question of where to take it," she said.

When Positive Thinking Doesn't Work

Some enduringly successful people keep a "positive attitude" regardless of the situation. These folks are rare. It's a helpful skill if you can muster it, but most Builders have a hard time choosing an attitude when they first hit a setback. Whether you're the president of a nation who loses after the first term or a manager or artist who gets a bad review, it hurts. What makes Builders different has to do with having a ThoughtStyle that moves them from negative emotion to constructive action quickly. It's what they eventually choose to do rather than how they feel about their recovery.

If it's not your nature to be able to flip a switch to "think positive," then thinking you should be able to won't help. Thinking positive may mean that you miss the opportunity to learn and get the full benefit of the insights to be gained from the failure or to understand what happened. The positive spin may even backfire, sending your emotions into a downward spiral because your mind has unfinished business. Builders go to work dealing with it directly instead of struggling to put a smile on their face. They don't pretend to be happy when things go wrong AND they refuse to completely surrender to the current disappointment. It's not that they feel good; they just harvest what they can from the setback and keep taking action.

"It's natural to feel like hell when things turn out badly," laughed Desmond Tutu, the Nobel Peace Prize-winning archbishop, sitting at the Waldorf Hotel on a frozen day in New York. He leaned forward, almost whispering, "But don't let that stop you. Emotions are a storm that sweeps through your life." This defeat you've had matters less than what you ultimately want to create, he said.

Builders don't try to "fix" that they feel badly; they believe that learning from the experience and getting on with their goal is the "fix." They feel the pain but cherish what they're building more than the misery of the moment—they believe their dreams deserve to be created and that they have an essential role in it, no matter how awful they feel today.

Despite the hazing, Builders shift their focus back to what they want to ultimately achieve—that thing they are committed to building. Instead of struggling to choose their attitude, they shift their focus to what works, and when they do that, their attitude improves as well!

Builders harvest failure. They turn their thoughts to understanding what happened so they can drive even faster without future wrecks. Sure, they focus most of their energy on passions and strengths, but they don't waste their mistakes by dismissing them. They put all of their experiences to use—the good, the bad, and the ugly.

> *Builders harvest failure.*

People like Dale Carnegie, Earl Nightingale, and Napoleon Hill were fathers of the self-improvement movement whose prolific advice about success could be considered a must-read when you've hit the wall. They were fascinated with harvesting failure, a treasure too often ignored by incessant denial and positive thinking. These guys make abundantly clear the idea that, if you haven't had lots of difficult challenges in your life, you're either not willing to admit it or you're not passionately engaged.

Why Yoda Is Actually Misunderstood

"Do or do not. There is no try," says Yoda, the bewitching philosopher warrior created by George Lucas in *Star Wars*. Yoda is quoted at least as often as the founding fathers on this topic.

Some complain that his philosophy doesn't equip you to survive a slump or recover from a mistake. In a culture that seems bent on perfection, entitlement, and instant gratification, it is often forgotten that most overnight successes require decades of failure to achieve their dreams. In Yoda's case, it sounds as though the aspiring Jedi Knight must magically summon the Force to do things perfectly the first time or not make the attempt.

"Quite the contrary," said Dr. Milton Chen, executive director of the George Lucas Educational Foundation, Edutopia. "The point of doing rather than trying is to make no mistake about your intentions. Your effort must be an intentional one—filled with sincerity and emotional commitment rather than half-hearted compromise," Chen said. "Pay attention to the quality of your offering. Do your best even though it may not be perfect or good enough today. Making a real effort is what makes it a valuable learning experience, not just the outcome."

Would You Be Willing to Learn if It Saved Your Life?

Failing an attempt at suicide at age 15, Jack dropped out of school. He had suffered a never-ending rollercoaster of depression and illness that left him secretly hoping that his life would end. There were no antidepressants, no magic prescriptions for Jack's condition. Suffocating migraines would send him into a panic in which he would lash out helplessly at everyone and everything. He once tried to set the house on fire and, during another episode, he chased his older brother with a butcher knife determined to kill him.

His family was "very poor," he said, but did their best to help. They had moved twice at the advice of doctors—first to drier, then to wetter climates—in search of an environment where the sickly teen could recover and grow.

Upon the advice of a friend, his mother took young Jack down to a lecture on improving one's health naturally. Embarrassed, he dragged his feet. By the time they arrived, the meeting hall was full. Jack felt relieved until the lecturer, nutritionist Paul Bragg, set two chairs out on the stage and said, "We don't turn anyone away."

Bragg focused on the trembling teen. "Do you want people to stop bullying you? Do you want the ladies to admire you?" Jack was captivated. The message would become his life's mission. Bragg recommended something that medical doctors at that time warned would cause heart attacks, hemorrhoids, and even impotence: It was called daily exercise.

This was 1929. The teen chose to change his life despite the warnings. As America's Great Depression deepened, it was perhaps reckless to start a business that conventional wisdom cautioned against. He would have to invent new ways of eating and new types of equipment that would make his exercise regimen possible. It was the beginning of a seven-decade career that is still going strong today. Jack La Lanne became the father of a revolution in health.

La Lanne faced and overcame many Tripping Points on his way to long-term success. He faced brutal public criticism to pursue his dream when traditional medicine thought it was dangerous. But it didn't start out as a revolution.

It was a recovery. In the beginning, he crawled from the depths of depression and debilitating illness. He started by getting off sugar and meat, and then creating a whole new way to think about feeding himself at a time when there were very few alternatives. At first, he wasn't able to muster the energy to do very much, but he inched forward, taking a small step—however tiny—each day to gather strength. His courage enabled him to save himself and, eventually, improve the lives of millions of others.

It's easy to do something because today we feel terrific, but skip it the day we feel badly. La Lanne still claims to hate exercise, although he hasn't missed a workout in 70 years. He "can't wait until it's over every day, but I'd be miserable if I didn't do it," he said. Why does he?

"Would you be willing to change," he shouted, "if it saved your life?" The feisty 92-year-old paced back and forth in his suite at the Sheraton Palace before his lecture at the Commonwealth Club as if he were still an excited teenager. La Lanne believes that a daily commitment to your passion, no matter how difficult, is the only way to enduring success.

When the Going Gets Tough, Feelings Come Last

Builders get back on course for the long haul because it matters more than their mood of the moment. Some psychologists call this externalizing the issue rather than taking it personally, or internalizing it. Wrong! Winners take it very personally—they just don't believe that the race is over. Professional athletes and coaches are popular authors on this topic because they are so familiar with a continuous process of losing and winning one play at a time in public.

"You can't change what you don't acknowledge," said Carl Lewis, Olympian of the Century. "What matters more than this one race is how to take the year. You feel lousy about your performance but you analyze what happened anyway and use that experience to win the next one."

Athletes, like pilots and sailors, tack left and right toward their dreams, never assuming they will get to their destination in a straight line. Builders don't obsess about the daily dilemmas. As the cliché goes, it's a marathon, not a sprint to enduring success.

There Is a Dark Side to Every Best Practice

One of the tripping points that make the adventure particularly difficult for people is what Builders describe as an overly self-critical tendency toward perfectionism and persistence for its own sake. Of course, both attributes are necessary and noble aspirations for which high achievers strive. It's true that you can't get much of anything done without perseverance. Stories of persistence making the vital difference are legendary and the pursuit of perfection is something to which many high performers aspire.

At the same time, an obsession for perfection is listed in the leadership and success literature as your worst enemy and persistence as your greatest asset. But perfection and persistence can both be just another addiction. We persist at all sorts of bad habits—like believing we must be perfect. Remember, drug addicts and alcoholics are persistent, too.

Builders achieve enduring success when they pour themselves into constructive habits—limiting their "addictions" to the passions that serve them.

The answer is neither perfection nor persistence, but obviously what to persist at. If the focus is on understanding meaning and learning from your tripping points, then there is growth. Builders achieve enduring success when they pour themselves into constructive habits—limiting their "addictions" to the passions that serve them.

Author Jack Canfield graduated from Harvard with a passion for helping kids whose self-esteem had been brutalized. He couldn't get publishers excited about his healing remedy for all ages. He churned through dozens of rejection letters for his first book until finally one publisher offered him tentative acceptance. He learned to persist at the right thing: Chicken Soup. Today he's coauthored more than 100 books in the famous *Chicken Soup* series and holds the Guinness World Record for seven *New York Times* bestsellers listed in the same week! For Canfield, what it's really about is having lasting impact on improving the lives of millions of people.

Losers Call It Failure; Winners Call It Learning

We apologize for the sappy clichés. Perhaps it's a blinding glimpse of the obvious. But, honestly, we heard it over and over and over again from Builders all over the world. People who have achieved enduring success drone on endlessly about learning from their mistakes.

When we complained about the trite nature of this idea to Quincy Jones, one of the biggest winners of Grammy Awards in history, we were sitting in a small study crammed with photos of celebrities in his hillside home perched above a smoggy Los Angeles. We had been trying all morning to hear ourselves think above the jackhammers pounding our ears from construction on a new house next door. The bone-rattling noise suddenly stopped for a moment and Q, as he likes to be called, sighed heavily and threw back another Bloody Mary. He pulled out a celery stick from his glass and crunched it for a moment:

"Shit yes, man, of course it's old news. You've got to get something out of everything that you fail at. But when was the last time you actually took that advice?"

Point taken. It's amazing how even the best ideas don't work if we don't actually put them to use.

You've Paid the Tuition, So Now Collect Your Payback

Every Builder said setbacks are to be searched for lessons. At a minimum, the lesson may be not to do the same thing again, or at least do it differently. Perhaps what becomes clear is how committed you are to doing what you're doing, allowing you to see different options that you wouldn't have recognized otherwise.[2]

What we heard from extraordinarily accomplished people was, "You've paid the tuition for failure, so it's time now to harvest the learning." Be greedy about wringing out every drop of useful content so you can do better next time. We use that emotionally charged word greed deliberately, because it shifts our ThoughtStyle from seeing a failure as just a liability to something that might be a transforming asset. Enduringly successful people told us to change our point of view about failure so that we could harvest everything that might actually be of use. Too often, people struggle with their embarrassment and leave it at that, or find themselves less confident about trying again.

In contrast, Builders use it all. Every experience teaches something. They don't use a weakness or a setback as a reason to distrust themselves. They don't marginalize themselves or the problem. If you fail to dissect the problem to see what is working and what doesn't—if you keep throwing away the experience—you may be doomed to repeat it.

Always Make New Mistakes

Technology pundit Esther Dyson's version of a pep talk is to say that anything worth doing will kick you into a constant state of trial and error, so take good notes as you stumble through. When you make mistakes, just "be sure to make new ones."

The auto industry is often known for resting on its laurels when business is going well, says Daimler Chrysler CEO Dieter Zetsche. Then when business falters, they scramble "to listen to customers and make things better." Success can make you sloppy and stupid if you allow it to, he said. Failure is a better teacher.

Builders think of both success and failure as feedback. They don't judge either as a complete win or loss. There is a gift and a warning in each one. We're not saying you shouldn't celebrate and mourn when it's appropriate. It's just that Builders don't jump to the conclusion that success is a prize awarded to us from others—as an entitlement—or that failure is a death sentence handed down from above that proves they are unworthy. Instead, Builders put the content to work for them. The question is not whether they won or lost this round, but what they will do with the feedback.

The Day I Blew Up The Factory

As we arrived at the corporate headquarters, a burst of wind sent the fall color swirling outside. The huge plate glass window of the conference room looked like an aquarium exhibit with the gold and scarlet leaves chasing all about. A short, balding man burst into the room and headed for the coffee service in the corner.

"We ta-ta-took longer than we thought," he stuttered, extending a warm handshake. The son of working class Irish immigrants, Jack Welch had a mother committed to boosting his confidence about everything, including stuttering, convincing him that his words couldn't possibly keep up with his intellect. The famed former CEO of General Electric (GE) was always the "shrimp" on the sports teams, as he would later describe himself. Perhaps a smaller stature fueled his enormous ambitions "to get out of the pile—define my own success and set myself apart from the crowd."

At 26, Welch landed his first leadership role at GE. Fresh out of school with a Ph.D., "I thought I was a pretty clever fellow," he admitted, but he never imagined that his first major achievement as lead engineer would be to blow up the factory. Welch recalls the "terrible explosion" when the chemical reactor flew through the roof, sending glass flying and employees sprinting from the building. The plant was trashed, but there was no serious damage to life, except Jack's shattered ego.

His boss said he should go tell his boss's boss what happened. "It was the longest drive and the longest night," Welch recalled. "I learned a lot from that experience. I went down to see him, told him what happened. He was a Ph.D. chemical engineer, professorial sort of guy, and all he was inquisitive about was what went wrong, and did I understand it, and what could I do about it, and could I design the commercial plant now that I'd blown up the pilot plant."

Welch said, "He did nothing but bolster my confidence—and he taught me something. I never ever go after anybody when they're down. Like, we even had jokes at GE about anybody who piles on—we threw the flag out—in meetings. Pull the white handkerchief out because it's just not something that we accept. Now, that doesn't mean if somebody is acting like a jerk some day some other way—and too cocky—we won't take him down a peg, but that's a different game."

A guy like Welch, never once accused of being a pushover, might not have learned that lesson so profoundly any other way.

Innovation Is Failure Sped Up

Builders find it irresistible to try, fail, improve; then try again, fail again, and get even better. The process summons

Darwin to mind as a common leadership metaphor. In theory, each generation rewards the winning mutations because they lead to survival, while the innovations that don't work never live to see another day. The only problem with drawing on Darwinism as a personal lesson for Builders is that natural selection leaves you, well, dead.

A better analogy might be capitalism, for all its flaws, which allows the entrepreneur to rewrite her DNA so that an entrepreneur or visionary can, even after bankruptcy, rise to try again with only the temporary sting of stigma attached. Amber Chand is just such an example. She deals in art—international handicrafts—which she locates, merchandises, and distributes all over the world.

In 1994, she ran across some beautiful baskets in Rwanda, in central Africa. "What was extraordinary about these baskets was that after genocide, when the country had been annihilated, 50 women got together under a tree—widows—their children had been macheted to death and their husbands had been killed. These women said 'either we will go mad with our pain or we will find a way to support each other.'" They were from the Hutu and Tutsi tribes—two groups that have been killing each other for decades.

"They had nothing. So they came together and they began to weave baskets. The baskets were such a symbol of what happens when people can come together and say, in spite of our differences, we must find a new way, we must find a way to build peace," Chand said. She called them the *peace baskets*.

"Subsequently, I made a commitment in Geneva that my company, Eziba.com, would do everything in its power to promote and present to the world the peace baskets of Rwanda to show that peace building is possible after the most devastating event and to show that women can be the emissaries of peace," Chand said.

"And this is the way women come to the peace table. They may not be sitting with the governments where they're not represented, but they are weaving and embroidering and stitching and coming together in their communities and finding ways to heal the community. As a business, I knew at that moment it was my responsibility and my company's responsibility to find a way to support that effort," she said.

"So for the Rwandan widows, who now are celebrating on the streets of Kigali, saying, 'Look! The baskets are selling out. We must be very talented. We didn't know that.' And suddenly you see this light go up in the faces of the people, saying, 'We are of value.' And that is when you can begin to see businesses thriving because it's almost like we are (providing) value and equality and respect as fundamental elements of the exchange of trade. And I said to them, 'My friends, if your baskets start showing poor quality, we're not going to carry them. And they go, 'Really?' And I say, 'We're a business. We're not a charity.' So that is the other piece of it."

A Great Cause and Almost Pointless Defeat

By 2004, ten years after starting Eziba, the company appeared to be growing. As the holiday gift-giving season approached, they scrambled to prepare for what is every retailer's biggest part of the year. Somewhere in the bowels of the organization, a manager accidentally selected a mailing list to send catalogs to the people least likely, rather than most likely, to buy Eziba's products. The mishap wasn't discovered until the deafening silence in the call center left them short of cash. The mistake sent Eziba into bankruptcy. The worst part, according to Chand, was the struggle to make sure that so many people, like those women making baskets, somehow got paid.

Two years later, she has re-launched a similar dream called The Amber Chand Collection: Global Gifts for Peace and Understanding. "This is the highest and most painful form of innovation," she sighed. "Our failure had nothing to do with a bad business or a bad idea. Why waste everything that we have worked so hard to learn? It deserves another chance."

Builders become more resolute after losing a battle they believe in because they learn from the loss—it gives them a better idea of what matters, what works, and what doesn't. Short-term "reality is an insult to the vision," said James G. March. "You have to be self-delusional to create change—it's a useful craziness guided or founded on your clear identity and knowing what you must do."

March is a retired professor of business, education, political science, sociology, and psychology, and author of six books of poetry. Nearly a decade after he last taught his course *Organizational Leadership* at Stanford, March distilled lifelong lessons into a film, *Passion and Discipline: Don Quixote's Lessons for Leadership*.

What can be learned from the fictional 16th-century *Man of La Mancha*, who haunted Spain, lashing out at windmills and challenging farm animals to battle?

"We live in a world that emphasizes realistic expectations and clear successes," March said in the film. "Quixote had neither. But through failure after failure, he persists in his vision and his commitment. He persists because he knows who he is." Quixote took the role of a noble knight who fought for honor and did things out of the "obligation of his identity, rather than relying on outcomes or consequences for a sense of self-worth."

That's the kind of stuff that Builders are made of—they put a way of life far above the importance of any one success or failure.

Hard Work Rewarded by Bad Headlines

Risk-takers and innovators are heralded as a good and rare breed. By definition, *innovation* requires a frequent iterative process of failure. Ironically, there is nothing socially acceptable or politically correct about failure. Almost nobody has patience for it. We idolize winners and demonize losers after a single game.

When Patricia Russo was installed in early 2002 as CEO of Lucent Technologies in Murray Hill, New Jersey, the bubble was just about ready to burst. Russo was among the group of career telecom executives who founded the technology networking company, backed by Bell Labs, in 1996. She had spent close to 20 years managing some of Lucent's and AT&T's largest divisions.

"In late 2000, things started to become challenging. And by 2002, the industry went into a totally unpredicted, unprecedented decline, whose depth and duration nobody was calling for. It felt like we were tap-dancing on quicksand; nobody could call correctly what was happening. If we knew then what we all learned a year later, we would have taken even more dramatic action sooner," she said.

Russo and her team have clawed their way back from losses, turning in Lucent's second consecutive profitable year when we spoke with her in 2005. Net income was over $1 billion on revenues of well over $9 billion.

During the crisis, she "was interviewed by a particular reporter I won't name, and it was very testy because the reporter was chastising our team rather aggressively about how difficult it had been for us to forecast our financial results."

"After a while, I stopped the interview and said, 'Do you think we're idiots?' He just looked at me. I said, 'This company has a lot of very capable people. We've got a lot of good history here. Do you think we're just stupid?'"

"He said, 'Well, no.' I said, 'Then there must be something else at play here that has created a phenomenon in the industry that makes it impossible to predict.' So I explained to him what had happened. And he said, 'You know what?

I didn't appreciate how the paradigm has shifted and what's different.' It was a very difficult time because the impression had been created that we just couldn't get it right, when the fact was that no one could. The industry simply had never experienced such a severe downturn," Russo said.

"Nobody anticipated what was happening, and we were all reacting to a target that was moving at a rate that we just couldn't imagine. All you can do in an environment like that is be open and honest about what's happening, what you know, what you don't know, what the risks are, and what the opportunities are. That's what we tried to do as we focused on the things we could control," she said.

The bad news is that even when you're doing your best, if you fail at any point, you'll get harsh reviews. Think of the last time you got good press for bad news. Nope. It's tough to find examples where public dialog ever refers to anyone's efforts as a noble failure.

This is not a complaint. We're not whining about the media. This is a reality check. You should not wonder why innovation doesn't happen in most organizations. For much of the journey, innovation is hard work rewarded by bad headlines.

This is just one more reason why people hide out from pursuing their full potential to follow their dreams and serve the world. Enduringly successful people aren't immune. They just tolerate the risks, feel the fear, take the brickbats, learn from failure, and do what matters to them anyway.

> *They just tolerate the risks, feel the fear, take the brickbats, learn from failure, and do what matters to them anyway.*

Tripping points are inevitable stumbles that Builders harvest. But even when complete recovery is not possible, as is the case for the people you're about to meet in the next chapter, there are powerful ways to prosper despite—and sometimes because of—the worst of circumstances.

The good news is that if you're willing to put up with the grief that comes from pursuing your dream, then congratulations. For better or worse, you've found what you should be doing with your life.

CHAPTER 8

Wounds to Wisdom—Trusting Your Weaknesses and Using Your Core Incompetencies

It's hard to fight an enemy who has outposts in your head.
—Yogi Sally Kempton

Things turn out best for the people who make the best of the way things turn out.
—John Wooden

His face was dominated by ungainly glasses with large lenses and geeky black rims. Every day, the fair-haired college freshman continued in his miserable struggle to keep up with his studies and classmates. Handicapped by learning disabilities, he had already flunked English and French. Growing up in Sacramento, he relied on classic comic books to make his way through reading assignments. That was no longer enough. Any courses that demanded critical reading and writing were simply overwhelming. For Chuck, it was a daily battle just to move his eyes across a page to absorb a little of what he read.

He dreaded the thought of anyone finding out the truth. But how could it be kept a secret any longer? He felt trapped. They were going to throw him out of school.

Chuck's challenge was thematic in the lives of heroes he would eventually have to study in Mythology 101. To succeed, he would also have to overcome formidable obstacles that loomed in his way. Actually, the most formidable obstacle was that he had to look in the mirror and face in himself what might be considered flaws fatal to success.

There Is No Cure

In the post-modern world, it has become human nature to expect our heroes to be perfect, despite overwhelming evidence that they never are. In the world of antiquity, the Greeks had no such expectations. To the contrary, it wouldn't be Greek mythology if the heroes weren't deeply flawed. And get this—there was no cure! If the hero failed to learn the lessons offered up by his flaws—well then—the story was a tragedy. Success didn't come from genius and rarely from talent. Only if the hero recognized the truth and wisdom in his weakness would the story end well. The plays of William Shakespeare were pretty much the same deal. If the heroes hit the *Aha!* moment before it was too late, the play was a comedy. If not, a tragedy. There were not that many comedies.

The lesson is always this: Weakness was not the cause of the tragedy; rather, the hero's relationship to the weakness became the cause of his undoing. At the heart of the hero's adventure was the idea that potentially tragic flaws or weaknesses must be embraced by the hero and included as elements of his authenticity—as part of who he was. To forget or deny this reality was the catalyst of tragedy.

In what passes for our civilized world, too many people spend too much time and too much money searching for "the cure," rather than getting on with building a life that matters. Worse still, if you do this, you could be trying to "cure" yourself of a virus for greatness!

Don't Use a Weakness as Reason to Distrust Yourself

Builders don't deny their flaws, nor do they allow them to paralyze action. They might feel embarrassed or overwhelmed by them at times, but they still don't marginalize themselves or the problem. They don't even "overcome" their "disability." They manage it, include it, cope with it, and don't let it stop them. In many cases, so called "disabilities" become embraced as the building blocks of greatness, of success that lasts.

You Can't Have It All Until You Use All You Have

In Chuck's case, he conceived of a way to include his dyslexia in his planning for life in many ways. First, he realized he could exchange his strengths with those of other people. He created a team—a study group of students who could be subject matter experts in each area of endeavor. The collected competencies rendered individual weaknesses less relevant. In fact, his team could get the work done even faster and more effectively than other teams with members who each believed they were experts at everything.

This once-floundering college freshman was Charles Schwab, now internationally known for reinventing financial services. The San Francisco-based firm that he founded in 1971, and which still bears his name, has more than a trillion dollars in customer assets.

What started out as an embarrassment were the seeds of Chuck's genius. Few captains of industry have the courage to admit it, but it's clear that many who have struggled with so-called learning disabilities have been among the most gifted CEOs, artists, and educators.

Among well-known dyslexic citizens, there are literally dozens of examples: George Washington, Agatha Christie, Albert Einstein, Woodrow Wilson, Winston Churchill, Thomas Edison, Nelson Rockefeller, Henry Ford, Walt Disney, William Hewlett, Paul Orfalea (founder of Kinko's), F.W. Woolworth, Alexander Graham Bell, Richard Branson, Cisco's John Chambers, CNN's Ted Turner, and dozens more who were quick to recognize what other leaders often take too long to learn: Their weakness can be an asset. For Chuck Schwab, his struggle forced him to get help and to rely on others to help him achieve his goals from the beginning. He never assumed—as many entrepreneurs do—that he was, or should be, good at everything.

"In some respects, the positive side of this learning issue thing was probably my early recognition that I wasn't strong in every component of reading, writing, and all those kinds of things," said Schwab.

"I could manage—with effort—the little chunks of text you see in a memo or a newspaper," Schwab said. "But a long book or a speech was almost impenetrable." Using a script for public speaking was often completely impractical for him. "The usual way you see a speech typed is all in uppercase, but for me that made every paragraph look like illegible gray blocks of type."

To cope, he would have each phrase typed in a different size and style—some large, some small—some bold, some underlined—"so when I looked down at the page, the words wouldn't all run together." By the end, what would look "like a ransom note to most people was much clearer for me," Schwab said.

Anyone who has seen Schwab speak in public or watched his nationally televised commercials might never notice his discomfort. "I won't do anything that I don't strongly believe in personally," Schwab insisted. His solution is to work hard at communication and speak from his heart rather than a script.

In school, he coped by getting focused on what he deeply cared about, then finding tutors and organizing study groups to get the work done. As an entrepreneur, he actively sought people who were not merely competent, but especially gifted to fill those organizational spots that Schwab himself could not.

"I knew from my own difficulties I needed to have other people who could complement me in different parts of the business that I was developing," he said. "I have been able, I think, to recognize my strengths and my deficits and build up around me a team of great people in the areas of deficit," he said. "I think that probably has been the single most important benefit that I received from having this learning issue early on in my life."

Cisco Systems CEO John Chambers sounds like a polished evangelical minister at the podium. But you won't find him reading a script. Those speeches are memorized. "I struggled in school and it was painful to read," he admitted. "My teachers thought I wasn't very smart and I wasn't sure either. I couldn't understand why I couldn't keep up."

His parents found the right tutors and, he sighed, "I had to work really hard." He dreaded the extra schoolwork, but his Spartan-like ethic helped him graduate second in his high school class, despite the fact that he, too, was dyslexic before there was a name for it.

Don't bother to send Chambers a long memo or ask him to write one. "It's a really laborious task," he said. This effervescent CEO avoids writing, choosing instead to see people and speak to them personally whenever possible. For Chambers, it's better to rely on humility than luck. His public appearances, web casts, and broadcasts reflect serious practice that consistently produces a compelling, clear message.

Chambers pain is Cisco's gain. He reaches out to his people and recruits customers around the world with energy and confidence that comes from years of doing it the hard way: "We prepare like we mean it and we never take the efforts of our employees or the challenges of our customers for granted—ever." Chambers can picture multiple dimensions of a problem even though it's tough to put pen to paper. "It's kind of second nature. I can visualize issues and make them clearer and simpler."

This may be genius, but it's also a matter of plain hard work and practice. Like the blind man whose hearing seems superhuman, leaders like Chambers have spent a lifetime honing the ability to turn complex ideas into simple, bold concepts as a way of coping with dyslexia. As told by Chuck Schwab: "Frankly, I don't have the luxury of leaving things complicated—I have to work every day at deciphering things for myself to make them clear. As it turns out, smart people like our customers hate overly complicated stuff, too!" For example, as he struggled to dissolve complexity in the mutual fund business, Schwab had an epiphany. "You don't have to have a problem with reading to have a problem reading a pile of mutual fund statements from ten different companies." Schwab's solution was to invent simple, one-stop shopping for mutual funds—a move that launched a new industry. "There has always been a huge opportunity in demystifying things for clients," Schwab insisted.

For decades, people like Chambers and Schwab kept their challenges a secret from the public. "I wasn't sure people would find my problem reassuring!" fellow dyslexic Richard Branson admitted. But ultimately, telling their story provided its own rewards. "I was amazed to see the impact I could have on the lives of people with learning differences," Schwab said. Both Schwab and Chambers have sponsored and led research efforts to help teachers and parents understand the problem.

The biggest dividend may be what the rest of us can learn from their struggle.

It's a difficult and nonintuitive step to think of the adversity that you are facing as an opportunity to actually find a

The biggest dividend may be what the rest of us can learn from their struggle.

way to make the challenge or the flaw itself somehow useful. There is a much bigger prize awaiting you. Like the hero or heroine, you may find that your perceived disadvantage may hold the seeds of your genius.

By embracing their pain, Builders gain something more powerful than just the ability to learn from mistakes or harness the value of persistence. It's even more than just empathy. Webster's dictionary defines empathy as "the action of understanding, being aware of, being sensitive to, and vicariously experiencing the feelings, thoughts, and experience of another of either the past or present without having the feelings, thoughts, and experience fully communicated in an objectively explicit manner."[1]

That doesn't quite capture it. The special knowledge and skill you can gain from painful personal experience seems to transcend even empathy. Builders who were once thought to have lost the genetic lottery and suffered learning disabilities have instead found that they won a prize: discovery of a special talent and a novel way to break out of the pack. This genius comes camouflaged one of two ways: As something that happens to you that in of itself cannot be changed—like a learning difference, for example, or something you made happen that went wrong that is irreversible except that it is still your responsibility to deal with it. Builders would not wish these potentially crippling challenges on anyone. If they happen to you, dig for the treasure where you fall, as philosopher Joseph Campbell writes. For most people, a stunning failure more often paralyzes than empowers. But for Builders, it's by far the most common form of pain that pays big dividends toward their lasting success.

When Tragedy Strikes

Young Govindappa Venkataswamy thought he had found his purpose in life when three cousins died in the last three months of their pregnancies. His broken heart drove him to devour his medical school training, bent on becoming an OB-GYN. His intent was to rescue people like his cousins, but he never got the chance. Fresh out of medical school, rheumatoid arthritis crippled him, making it impossible for him to deliver babies. He was hospitalized for years and suffered pain that still grips him to this day.

"You don't spend your life helping people just out of sympathy. You know that the sufferer is part of you," said Dr. V., as he is known today. Not only does he have great empathy for the pain that his patients endure, but he did not let his permanent disability limit his ambitions. He started over, this time studying ophthalmology to confront a different need. In India, there are nine million blind people—most of whom suffer from cataracts, which are curable with surgery.[2] Dr. V. opened an 11-bed eye hospital in his brother's home in Madurai to perform free or low-cost cataract surgery. He even designed instruments suited to his crippled hands, and these tools enabled him to perform 5,000 surgeries in his first year.

Today, his clinics perform over 200,000 surgeries annually and are among the largest single providers of eye surgery in the world, having given sight to more than one million people in India. Dr. V made the process of conducting operations so efficient, it could be done as fast and almost as cheaply as making a burger.

He believes that it may be possible to "franchise" his operations throughout the world, recruiting people and resources to his dream as if it were McDonald's. They sell billions of burgers through thousands of stores, he tells everyone he meets. "We can sell millions of people new eyesight, saving them from starvation." The clinics run a profit even though 70% of the patients pay nothing, or close to nothing, and the clinics do not depend on donations or government grants. With his hands hopelessly crippled, you would think he had earned the right to give up. Instead, Dr. V refused to let that interrupt his commitment to save lives. He could not change his condition, but he could change the way he thought about his goal and, as a result, he is changing the lives of millions.

Greatness Comes at the Intersection of Pain and Passion

Dr. V's selfless courage in India cannot help but remind us of Mahatma Gandhi. Consider for a moment the journey of this talismanic icon for peace and freedom. It turns out that had Gandhi not encountered pain in his early years out of college, he might not have transformed his view of the world enough to change history. Gandhi might have settled into a nice, quiet law practice were it not that his overwhelming fear of public speaking forced him to make other plans. Enduringly successful people have found that the answer to their life's purpose is buried not in passionate love or pain alone, but in the struggle over both together, working in strange harmony.

Gandhi studied law in London, and he loved the idea that the law could settle divisive issues, though on his return

> *Enduringly successful people have found that the answer to their life's purpose is buried not in passionate love or pain alone, but in the struggle over both together, working in strange harmony.*

to India, he rarely saw it used that way. His passion was real, but in the courtroom, he found himself unable to speak. He left Bombay feeling defeated.

When he was offered a job in South Africa as counselor for a Muslim business, he was delighted. As it turned out, the journey to Pretoria changed his life. He was ejected from a train compartment even though he held a first-class ticket, was beaten for refusing to give up a seat on a stagecoach, and was kicked from a path by a policeman. Indians living in South Africa could not vote, own homes, go out at night without a permit, or walk along a public path. Gandhi's understanding of their plight was intense and personal. His growing anger summoned a new voice he had never experienced before. *The cause had charisma.* He may have been speechless in the courtroom, but the pain of his people helped him discover his life's purpose.

Pain Had Finally Freed His Passion

He decided to do things on his day job differently, too. While Gandhi began gathering petitions to emphasize the plight of Indians in South Africa, he at the same time worked on the legal case that brought him there in an entirely new way. Instead of the normal legal fistfight, Gandhi pushed for arbitration. The parties agreed and, in fact, the arbitrator decided the case in favor of Gandhi's employer. But he didn't stop there. Even though he had won his case, he pressed his client to accept small incremental payments that saved face, allowed for dignity, and prevented bankruptcy for the case's loser.

This two-way respect of adversaries—his insistence on "win-win" creative solutions to all sides of a conflict—tapped a passion deep inside him that was the reason he had been drawn to practice law in the first place. It became his fundamental concept—*satyagraha*, or "holding to the truth."

From then on, in hundreds of instances, it was Gandhi's practice to try to bring about a compromise outside of court rather than to drive for a crushing victory. He had found a way back to his passion for the law, and it came from the pain he suffered over the discrimination of all oppressed people. The two together were a powerful alchemy that sustained him through prison, strikes, and social conflicts—from the fair treatment of "untouchables"—to the freedom of India itself.

Pain or Passion Will Make You Good Enough— Pain + Passion Will Point You to Greatness

Although it may seem strange that we'd rely on pain so much as a part of the big picture, Builders have found it to be unavoidable on their road to lasting success. As revealed in the previous chapter, they feel they might as well get some good out of it. But pain may give you more clarity than your passion. The question is, why do we care about what we care about? We don't care just because we enjoy doing something. There are many things that we enjoy or even lust after, but few provide lasting success.

There are many things we dislike, too, so just finding what eats you is not the answer either. What adds to the mystery is that not all successful people have the same definition of what is painful, just as they don't really have the same definition of success or happiness. For most things in life, we can't assume that what hurts each of us is universal, so here is some insight to the upside of pain. What we consider to be painful offers a window to our soul—to see uniquely who we are and what we must do.

Do you love to play music and at the same time find it disturbingly painful to hear a flat note on that CD, or hate to live without music for a whole day? Let's forget for a moment that friends and relatives think it's foolish or even dangerous for you to choose music as your next profession. Do you love to write poetry and find it torturous to read a bad sentence? When I say painful, I don't mean annoying— I mean, does it torment you, keep you awake at night, or get you up in the morning?

When novelist Tom Robbins was asked by a journalist what was the most important thing in the world for him, he simply said, "A good sentence."

These two examples mean something to anyone who cares about music or writing, but may seem trivial to anyone who does not. That's part of the test.

Letting Go of What Doesn't Work

At its highest and best level, perhaps that horrible thing in your life—that failure or disability or source of outrage—is the genius. Gandhi could not have found his voice without pain; CEOs Schwab, Chambers, and Branson could not have built their companies without their dyslexia. By their nature, Builders are obsessed with creating or building something—and they're on a never-ending quest for something of value they can use. When it comes to their flaws, nothing goes to waste.

One of the things that Builders do discard quickly is blame. When you talk with them, what is clearly missing is the natural human tendency to dwell on blaming other people and things for our problems. Builders may explode, grieve, and (privately) blame everything and everyone, but most appear to drop it quickly. Instead, they look at what they can change and deal with that directly without prolonged whining. Wallowing in blame of yourself or others doesn't actually deal with the problem or allow progress toward the goal.

Builders let go of what doesn't work when it isn't working. They don't make the future pay the debts of the past. They don't make the next job, or next company, or next lover, pay for their last bad experience. You don't win by punishing the next boss for what you didn't get from the last one. You can't let the past invent your future.

Billionaire Jon Huntsman, author of *Winners Never Cheat*, learned this lesson on his first job. "My employer in the first business in which I worked was always in a rage over competitors," he said. "We were in the egg-processing business. He continually schemed on how to make the competition fail. He wasted so much effort on this mission that his company suffered. He insisted his staff fabricate stories about the competition with the news media. He concocted every negative thought and trick possible to make his competitors fail." Huntsman could feel how much that drained his energy and everyone else's around him. It wasn't worth it. His boss "died a pathetic, virtually bankrupt individual,"[3] he says. Huntsman vowed that he would never waste his life that way.

> *Builders let go of what doesn't work when it isn't working. They don't make the future pay the debts of the past.*

Case Dismissed

Builders eventually make the choice to let it go not because they're in denial, but because they must keep focused on what they're building. It's not that everything was forgiven, or that the pain was completely healed, or that all the injustices that may have happened to them have been ignored. They do not try to rewrite history or to wipe the slate clean. They don't pretend it didn't happen. They simply decide to dismiss the case and move on. Obsessing on grudges keeps them alive; letting them go forces them to die as you get back to business.

Some call this "completion" or "forgiveness," but that implies that there is absolution, resolution, or restitution—or at least an adequate apology. Unfortunately, when bad things happen, much of what happens is rarely completely resolved or healed. But, nevertheless, Builders find a way to move on anyway so they can create the future. The root of the word "forgive" is actually *to send away*—to dismiss.

"'Dismiss' is a very strong word," said Reverend Deborah Johnson. "When something is dismissed, it's over. When it's dismissed, you don't keep going back to it." That's what successful people do. They don't necessarily call it forgiveness, but they do abandon blame as a way of life.

"Now, there's a funny thing about this notion of dismissing the case. When you're in a court of law and, at some point, the judge says 'case dismissed,' that doesn't mean case erased. There will still be a record of the case in the books. But what isn't going to happen is we're not going to keep going through the particulars of this case. Dismissed doesn't mean that all the parties in it experience resolution. It doesn't even mean that a crime didn't take place." When the judge dismisses the case, it's because there will be no more prosecution at this point. "It's over," she insisted.

Do we want to build for success or hang on to conflict? Which of these choices do extraordinarily successful people invest in for the long term? Do they spend their days committed to creating *conflicts built to last* or *success built to last*? When you become willing to let it go, the cycle is broken and you have freedom. Case dismissed.

"What this requires most is that we let go of the story of what happened and our attachment to it. When you let it go, you're not dragging your past with you into your future. When you let it go, you're seeing that you're bigger than what's happened to you," the Reverend contended.

During the Holocaust in World War II, 15-year-old Elie Wiesel had no real hope of escape. He was packed like cold meat in railcars with family, friends, and neighbors, and delivered to Auschwitz. Within moments of his arrival at this infamous concentration camp, he was put in line with his father to march toward open pits where he witnessed the Nazis throw babies and shove children and adults at gunpoint to burn alive. Two steps from the precipice, he was momentarily spared. He would miraculously endure three years of horror that he describes in his brilliant and terrifying book, *Night*. By the time the Allies arrived, Wiesel's mother, father, and a younger sister were among the millions of Jews who had been brutally tortured and murdered.

He had every reason to be consumed by hatred. The case against the Nazis will never be dismissed. Still, Wiesel dedicated his life to peace and recovery, winning the Congressional Gold Medal in 1985 and the Nobel Peace Prize in 1986. "Hate will destroy you," he said. The lifelong mission he set in motion for himself and his Foundation is "to combat indifference, intolerance, and injustice through dialogs and youth-focused programs that promote acceptance, understanding, and equality."

Beyond Blame—Creating a Future That Matters

What makes Wiesel's lesson so especially difficult is that under harsh circumstances, it takes tremendous courage and wisdom not to cast oneself as a victim and leave it at that. And, as a victim, your chances of ever making a lasting positive impact on the world are slim.

Builders claim that it's your choice to decide whether to be the victim or a beneficiary of what there is to harvest from the most difficult circumstances.

Joe Nichols, Jr., will tell you he had to make exactly that kind of choice. "At 20, my life was a train wreck. I had no

Builders claim that it's your choice to decide whether to be the victim or a beneficiary of what there is to harvest from the most difficult circumstances.

future," Nichols said. The soft-spoken, 41-year-old entrepreneur from Houston insisted, "No one would ever hire me because it was unlikely I'd ever be able to do much of anything." Eventually, with his family's encouragement, he finished college, and together they started a small mail stop.

Business was brutal through those first few years. During the long, challenging work days of these early years, Joe found himself a little envious of all the exotic places that his parcels would travel to and arrive from, dreaming that some day he might have the opportunity to visit far-flung romantic destinations. "But in my situation, I was never likely to leave the state of Texas, let alone travel the globe."

Eventually, he expanded the store, opened a second one, then a third, and 16 years later, the family business now has a profitable chain of franchises across Texas, Louisiana, and Arkansas. As Hurricane Katrina descended on the New Orleans location last year, his family scooped up all their employees and brought them to Houston. (The team was kept safe and sound—and they were out of business for only four hours!)

Nichols and his family were showered with accolades, "but I don't know that our actions warrant a pat on the back. There was simply no other choice in those circumstances," he insisted. "Opening our doors was the natural thing to do and we know that others would do it for us if the tables were turned."

Today, the Nichols extended family is the millionaire next door, and Joe was, for many years, an active leader in the Texas Jaycees. He is passionately committed to helping others build their lives despite all odds, and loves to recruit celebrities for events to raise funds for people in need, although his wife teases him about how it sounds like bragging when he drops names at social events.

"So how did you do it?" Mark Thompson asked him during dinner.

"Are you asking about fundraising or our business?" he laughed. At that moment, they were interrupted by the sommelier as he emptied the last of the Moet & Chandon into their glasses, followed closely by three waiters bearing desserts to simultaneously present to each of us, after setting them aflame. They were on the last day of a five-star cruise along the Mexican Riviera.

"No," Mark continued. "How did this happen to you, Joe?" He was looking at the wheelchair.

Joe Nichols nodded, and his wife, Bonnie, reached for his glass of champagne, pressing it against his fingers and pushing it to his lips. He used a brace on his right hand to spoon his meal into his mouth, but he needed to ask for help every time he wanted a drink. He had become a quadriplegic in an automobile accident, confined to a wheelchair long before he built a thriving business and even found his wife, Bonnie, with whom he now has two kids.

It was just past sunset on a little country road on February 18, 1984. Nichols swerved to miss oncoming traffic on a slick turn after a rainstorm. His car plummeted into a ditch and rolled. He remembers seeing the fire trucks and ambulance descend on him in the darkness. The friend who was riding with him had gotten out with barely a scratch. But when they pushed the car off its side, Joe Nichols fell through the driver-side window in a limp twisted pile of flesh and limbs. "As a quadriplegic, it seemed like life would stop," he recalled.

You may have the same burning question that we did. Who was at fault in this terrible accident?

He shook his head. "The reality is that I'm in a wheelchair. The more important question now is not who is to blame, but who is responsible for what. I'm responsible for my life."

Nichols holds himself accountable to his chosen ThoughtStyle, responsible for creating what might still be possible despite his circumstances and because it matters—not languishing in despair because of his circumstances and despite what matters.

"Now if I told you it was my fault, then I would be the victim of my own error." He had obviously given this speech before. "And if it was someone else's fault, then that would give me the space to be a total victim."[4] Joe figured out there was no future in either position.

"Sure, at first I went through a long period of pain and the full range of grief—the horrible loss of 'who you used to be,'" he said. "Sometimes, I'd have spasms that would terrify my wife, sending me out of control, off the bed and onto the floor. A few times I'd be in class at the University of Texas and my bladder would let go. Mom would pile books in my lap and race me home. There I was, 21-years old and my mother is still changing me. There were many humiliating moments, but I guess what you do is keep going one more day—no matter how miserable you might be. Eventually, the pain lessens and you realize you're still here—you're still alive—and what you thought was impossible last month, well, you're doing that now. All of that builds confidence."

The overwhelming lesson we took away from Joe Nichol's courageous journey is that assuming the role of the victim just leaves one paralyzed in a state of learned helplessness, waiting for someone or something other than ourselves to make it right. That's not how Builders think. Nichols has remarkable strength, but in one respect, he's like every Builder we've ever met. He holds himself accountable to what he wants to create rather than wallowing in shame or blame about what's happened. His words, intentions, and behaviors all relentlessly focus on creating a desired future.

Some things cannot be overcome. Many things have no cure. But they can be managed and put to use just as Joe Nichols does. They can be turned from wounds into wisdom by never wasting a moment of what is left of his life—never taking tragic comfort in a victimized belief that he cannot make a difference. He knows that he can.

When you don't have the use of your arms and legs, every ounce of effort has to count, so this man spends his energy thinking how he will continue to build a successful life for his family, his employees, and his community. No matter how bad things get or how horrible he feels, people like Joe Nichols show us what is possible—and take from us our hiding places.

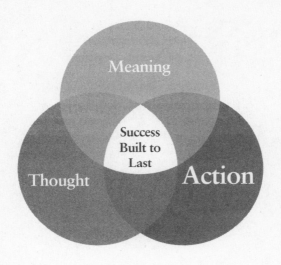

PART III

ActionStyles—Turning Passion into Action

About Action—earning your luck by turning Passion into Action * Achieving the alignment you need * Enjoying a life that matters

---

"Anything worth doing cannot be done alone."

Earning Your Luck—Preparing for Serendipity by Using Big Hairy Audacious Goals

Nothing is more difficult than to introduce a new order.
Because the innovator has for enemies all those who
have done well under the old conditions and lukewarm
defenders in those who may do well under the new.
—Noccolo Machiavelli

I am a great believer in luck, and I find the harder I work,
the more I have of it.
—Thomas Jefferson

If you ask enduringly high achievers about their success, most will tell you it was a serendipitous journey. That is not to say they were just lucky. In 1754, Horace Walpole, the fourth Earl of Orford, England, coined the term *serendipity,* based he said on "a silly fairy tale called *The Three Princes of Serendip*, in which the heroes were always making discoveries, by accidents and sagacity, of things which they were not in quest of...."[1]

In the tropical paradise of Serendip, which roughly translates as "island where the lions live," a powerful king named Giaffer tests his sons by separately inviting them to take his place on the throne. One at a time, each prince, with grace and respect that exceed their years, turns their father down. Although the king was amazed by their wisdom, he was not done with them. Convinced that the princes needed real-world experience, he banished them from the kingdom.

Not exactly what you would call a serendipitous journey so far, and indeed, their "luck" did not improve. No sooner did the princes arrive on the first leg of their adventure when a camel shepherd interrupted them to ask if they have seen one of his dromedaries. They hadn't, but like detectives, they came up with a detailed description of the camel based on clues they had noticed along the way.

The princes amazed the camel driver "by asking him if the lost camel is blind in one eye, missing a tooth, and lame."[2] The princes also said the camel "carried a load of butter on one side and honey on the other, and was ridden by a pregnant woman." The princes appeared to be so familiar with the camel that the driver concludes they have stolen the animal, and he has the unsuspecting princes thrown in jail. It is only after the driver's neighbor finds the camel that they are released.

As the fantastic story circulates, the Emperor Beramo summons the princes to his palace. He asks them how they could give such an accurate description of a camel they had never seen. The princes dismiss any magic solution. It was logic and a keen eye. The princes had cleverly solved the mystery based upon the evidence, in a Sherlock Holmes sort of a way.

The royal trio went on to have many more challenges and solved each one, winning treasures they could not have imagined in the beginning of their adventure.

You Earn Your Luck

Actually, this fable is more about earning your luck than simply getting lucky—a fitting metaphor for the rocky and unpredictable road that Builders tread to pursue their dreams. The overwhelming majority of Builders claim that their success has been a serendipitous journey, and the luck they enjoyed was usually earned, often at great cost. They have done that by focusing on doing work that is meaningful to them and going deep to discover relevant clues along the way. They set big goals and engaged completely in the work at hand.

As a consequence, Builders are better prepared to turn things that, on the surface, may seem bad or useless into opportunities. What may appear to be brilliance, heroism, or passive good luck is actually a saga of passion, depth, and skill. Because they love what they do, Builders invest the time to acquire detailed knowledge about things that matter. It is focus and knowledge more than brains or brawn that allows them to observe the subtleties of their path and then take advantage of serendipitous events. Like the princes in the story, Builders describe their path as adventures filled with bad breaks and unplanned good fortune. Only a prepared mind and open heart prevails.

> *Like the princes in the story, Builders describe their path as adventures filled with bad breaks and unplanned good fortune.*
> *Only a prepared mind and open heart prevails.*

Are Builders Saying Goals and Plans Are Pointless?

No, they are often essential. In fact, Builders use planning and goals—often big goals—to put themselves into a serendipitous position. In *Built to Last*, Collins and Porras coined the phrase Big Hairy Audacious Goals (BHAGs) to describe how visionary organizations drive boldly toward their aspirations based on their core values. BHAGs don't just exist in parallel to your ideology; they are a manifestation of it. They are an extension of who you are and what matters to you.

"To set Big Hairy Audacious Goals requires a certain level of unreasonable confidence. Like (President Kennedy's) moon mission, a true BHAG is clear and compelling and serves as a unifying focal point of effort—often creating immense team spirit," they say.[3] And like the moon, the goal even outlives its creator, as the space race lost no momentum after the president's assassination. He never saw Neil Armstrong set foot on the lunar surface, but the goal had already galvanized the nation.

"A BHAG engages people—it reaches out and grabs them in the gut. It is tangible, energizing, highly focused. People 'get it' right away; it takes little or no explanation. It has a clear finish line, so the organization can know when it has achieved the goal; people like to shoot for finish lines."[4] These BHAGs involve a consistent pattern of making bold, risky investments in audacious projects—to stimulate forward progress while still preserving core values and ideology.

The Myth of Authenticity

BHAGs give you something tangible to be authentic about. Much has been said about the need for leaders to be authentic, but Builders will tell you to be careful about what that means. Your BHAG must be 'real,' but the world doesn't want to know everything you're thinking.

The battle cry for authenticity is a well-intentioned call to action that takes subtle judgment in its execution. In other words, you are well advised to summon the courage to demonstrate that you are honestly connected to the goal.

Your behavior has to match your words. And your words should take the form of personal stories rather than clever quotes from heroes you've never met. For anyone to give a damn about what you're recruiting them to do, people want to know the skin you have in the game. You've got to find your own way to express the passion and personal meaning you have invested in this goal or mission.

On the other hand, even Churchill—the twentieth-century leader who is most often quoted in canned pep talks—wasn't authentic all the time. Churchill didn't reveal his doubts about Britain's survival during World War II when those possibilities crossed his mind. Nor did he dwell in public on his predilection for heavy drinking and womanizing. Neither Churchill nor Lincoln obsessed in public over the nagging depression that dogged them throughout their extraordinary careers. Nor does America want to know about a bad day the president might be having.

Too Much Presidential Information

To thine own self be true. But which self should you be true to? You are a man or a woman, a son or daughter, a student and teacher, a lover and loved one. As explored in *Portfolio of Passions*, you are likely to have many passions. You don't have to have multiple personalities disorder to experience different selves when you pursue those passions, and some of them are nobody else's business. Hazel Markus, a cognitive psychologist, noted, "There isn't just one you; you have many selves packaged up in your various roles in life."

Jimmy Carter was criticized in the media for his honest admission to *Playboy Magazine* that he had felt lust for a woman, even though by definition that's authentic and unavoidable if you are a healthy heterosexual male. His intention was to reassure folks that they could think "naughty" passing thoughts and still choose to behave in ethically and spiritually driven ways. But Carter's empathy was not judged appropriate to his role, nor did it advance his mission as president of the United States and leader of the Free World.

It's incredibly unfair, perhaps. The reality is that some parts of your authentic self are better off left in the shadows if they are not useful and relevant in directly supporting or furthering your goals and establishing the integrity of your objectives. This is where BHAGs can provide the boundaries to keep you from straying from your message.

Martin Luther King, Jr., anchored his life's purpose and inspired the world with his indelible dream. By brilliantly articulating his audacious goal and steadfastly living his values, King, with a compelling clarity of vision, led a transformation of humanity's perception of what was possible. In some respects, his impact has been greater than even he planned. King did not set out to create his permanent legacy in world history. He did have the courage of his convictions and create lasting change.

Rev. King also achieved less than he hoped for—racial discrimination still lurks in shadows in every society. But the power of his goal will forever empower progress in the human condition.

Rabbi Israel Singer of the World Jewish Congress said, "Our beliefs are our assets and our liabilities. Our choices make the difference about whether they hurt or help our cause." He has spent a career working with rabbis, popes, and cardinals—helping to build a bridge between Judaism and Christianity. Rabbi Singer's goal to bridge the faiths is big, hairy, and audacious. And today, he's seeking to bring together Jewish, Christian, and Islamic clergy to join in dialog.

"It's not like we're just do-gooders. Some people believe the world is fixable, which is nice; but we believe in incremental and small wins that add up to permanent change. That's the way to make a difference," he contended.

"It's really important not to get discouraged" that you're not achieving your goal right away, he says. BHAGs don't just become valuable for the first time when they are achieved—their first value is in defining the journey. It's "what happens to you along the way that matters—how you are changing as you change the world," Rabbi Singer insisted.

"Your influence may seem relatively small at the moment, but it's all the little steps that stack up to high impact. You change the world person-by-person, town-by-town, rabbi-by-rabbi, priest-by-priest, minister-by-minister, imam-by-imam, denomination-by-denomination; one idea and one life at a time."

The Explorer Mentality

No matter how grand their ambitions, Builders like Singer did not imagine how different their success might be from their plans, nor did they have a roadmap in their pocket that resembles the path that they took. Their goals help them build a vision and create a "way of life that they are seeking." But if you could have asked them 20 or 30 years ago to describe the life that they hold in their hands today, very few could have done it.

Steve Jobs' aforementioned vision to put a computer on every desk was realized, but Apple wasn't the company that delivered 95% of those machines. Gandhi never achieved his goal to unify the Hindus and Muslims, but few have done more to create peace and freedom than this man with a loving vision.

For most Builders, the journey is like shooting for the moon and instead hitting Mars—perhaps a better, but different, outcome than envisioned. Had they not been prepared to explore in the first place, they would not have been able to hit a better target. Builders are the first to admit (at least, in private) that planning works, but as the adage goes, the plan itself rarely does. While it's hard to make progress without planning, Builders find that what they seek in the long term doesn't always turn out as expected.

Publisher Steve Forbes advised that one of the most important "things you have to be prepared for in life is serendipity." He said, "You may be looking for something but you may end up with something else if you have your eyes open." Forbes shared the classic example of Ray Kroc, the man who created McDonald's. He was in his fifties in a so-so career as a milkshake machine salesman when he stumbled across this hamburger stand run by the McDonald Brothers and said, "My God, if they expand, I can sell them more milkshake machines." But when the McDonald Brothers didn't think the business should expand the way Kroc envisioned, he bought them out and the rest, as they say, is history. Indeed, for Builders who stay true to what they know and what matters to them, things actually have a knack of turning out better than they imagined, Forbes said.

> *Indeed, for Builders who stay true to what they know and what matters to them, things actually have a knack of turning out better than they imagined.*

This is one of the more subtle, but critical, powers of BHAGs. They instantly capture your heart and head. They deliver clear direction. Don't confuse direction with a roadmap, however. Builders have the former, but not the latter. Take the race to the moon, for example. What is often forgotten is that when the BHAG of "a man on the moon and back before the end of the decade" was conceived, America had no clue how to actually accomplish this.

The meaning of the mission was not in the moon or the pretense that we knew how to get there. The moon is just a lump of rock that messes with earth's gravity, tides, and our mood swings. The meaning of the moonshot was in our audacity to consider an actual journey to this remote and mystical place. Kennedy's declaration stirred the nation's competitive spirit. Science became a metaphor for the triumph of democracy over totalitarian communism. It wasn't that we knew how to do it, but that we believed we had to do it.

This is frankly how most Builders live their lives, and it is the secret to lasting success. It's all about meaning first and method second. Although scientists had some ideas about how to approach a lunar launch, no one had anything close to total knowledge about how to get there and back, particularly Kennedy. The direction was clear, but there was no blueprint. The BHAG itself was a container for America's dream; it became the context for driving progress, bridging the gap between uncertainty and reality. BHAGs help you survive that kind of ambiguity. The moon-shot BHAG helped Americans tolerate an unreasonable, overwhelming and excruciatingly detailed course of action and have the patience to chart out what basic measurable steps could be taken to get there. It gave a country uncharacteristic courage to swallow public failures, learn from them, improve, and eventually prevail through thousands of tiny steps.

Bold Risks Measured in Small Steps

Builders take bold risks that they measure in small steps. That's what Rabbi Singer is doing. That's what Michael Dell has always done.

"I would characterize the start up of the company as a series of experiments," Dell said, pointing to the white board where he had listed noble ideas that missed the mark. "Most of which failed, but none of which were large enough disasters to destroy the company."

Most people don't do well with ambiguity. Builders do. Ambiguity is the enemy of audacity and innovation. It strikes fear in our heart and doubt in our heads. When was the last time you were able to sell an idea to your boss, your partner, or your team without an exact battle plan for getting it done? Did they not want a detailed process for getting there, and certainty about the outcome?

It's human nature to crave certainty and repudiate ideas that don't have guarantees. And yet, very few things do. Great ideas and great careers don't have perfect plans before launch date.

Michael Dell had just this sort of BHAG. It was clear and confident, with a paucity of detail or certainty. But that is not how it looks when you read about Dell. The press gushes over him as if he found a chest hidden in his freshman dorm room containing the treasure map for his life.

If you've met Michael, however, he is a self-effacing, down-to-earth guy who reassures you that he had no precise plan. He just dared to go where no one has gone before. The compelling nature of the idea or goal, not the plan, is what launches entrepreneurs. Dell realized he could bypass retail stores and sell his computers to consumers direct by mail—and got almost instant validation—netting a cool $80,000 in his first year. Not surprisingly, he opted for selling computer equipment out of his bathtub at University of Texas, Austin, instead of getting a college degree.

In the time he would have taken to earn a sheepskin, he became the youngest person to take a company public on the stock market. But within a year, he faced disaster when his warehouses overflowed with excess inventory of electronic components. The enthusiasts' package of computer technology he thought would sell bombed with consumers. Although Dell is known for his big idea about bypassing traditional retail stores, he desperately needed to clear excess inventory. It very nearly killed the company until he decided to distribute through CompUSA and Best Buy stores for awhile, temporarily violating his BHAG to sell only by mail.

No sooner did he get things back on track when the firm hit the wall again. Dell struggled with losses in a business that would prosper later—laptops—and he also faced costly mistakes in Europe. He was forced to cancel a second public offering to the stock market.

Clawing his way out of this second big slump, *Upside* magazine named Dell turnaround CEO of the year, and he delivered a line that has become legendary: "I hope I don't ever win that award again!"

Responsible Chutzpah or Audacious Accountability

Like most Builders, what Dell had going for him on this roller coaster ride was an odd mixture of accountability AND audacity. It's tough to find the right word for this leadership quality. The Yiddish dictionary gets closer: We're talking about a responsible form of *chutzpah*—the non-conformist gutsy audacity to create something despite all odds, for better or for worse. In this case, responsible chutzpah leaves out the completely self-absorbed arrogance associated with the word.

Leo Rosten in *The Joys of Yiddish* defines chutzpah as "gall, brazen nerve, effrontery, incredible 'guts,' presumption plus arrogance such as no other word and no other language can do justice to."[5] The difference here is that long-term Builders are accountable—they are people who deliver for themselves and the outside world at the same time. Accountability means "to stand and be counted, as a part, a cause, an agent, or a source of an event or set of circumstances." Audacious accountability means you consider your life from the point of view that how it goes and what happens is up to you. Don't worry; this is not an infomercial for so-called human potential movement psychobabble. This is one of best lessons from human history: You may or may not be to blame for what happens to you, but either way you are responsible for doing something about it.

> *This is one of best lessons from human history: You may or may not be to blame for what happens to you, but either way you are responsible for doing something about it.*

Builders don't claim to feel in total control, but they do have the audacity to embrace the idea that they alone (or with the help of a Creator) are building this life for a reason, rather than life being something that happens to them while they're making other plans.

If this sounds like a contradiction in terms—if you feel a paradox, oxymoron, or even a paradigm shift coming your way here—then you're right. In fact, very few long-term achievers would describe their personal goals as being audacious or demanding Herculean accountability, per se.

For Lasting Success, Size Doesn't Matter

Unlike the bold visions they may paint for their organizations, Builders do not describe what drives them personally as big, hairy, or audacious. Size doesn't matter. The scope of the goal and its relative audacity were irrelevant to them, or perhaps they just preferred not to think in those terms.

In fact, there was a definite sense of naïve enthusiasm to many of these conversations that transcends logic and is certainly beyond the scope of conventional thinking. These people viewed what they were doing with a Zen-like air that makes you wonder whether one of the reasons they could pull off such audacious achievements was because they just didn't see them as all that audacious!

In *Built to Last*, Collins and Porras found that "BHAGS looked more audacious to outsiders than to insiders. The visionary companies didn't see their audacity as taunting the gods. It simply never occurred to them that they couldn't do what they set out to do."[6]

Very few Builders even gave their work an intimidating label like a Mission, Calling, Cause, or Higher Purpose. Such a pedestal can develop as an unnecessary torment. Indeed, Builders describe their objectives as essential—that it must be done—that it deserved to happen. They believed it was serious, the right thing to do; a better way. It was what they had to do now. It was long term, but urgent.

Builders tell you about the joyful and painful accidents that lead to a full life. It's extremely important, however, to emphasize here that they are very picky about which serendipitous events they choose to pursue. They only go after that which means a great deal to them—stuff they love or find painful to ignore—something that matters so much they find the courage to engage, despite the opinions of others, not because of them.

Builders don't set up preachy descriptions that might unwittingly create any more barriers to success than those already lurking out there. Instead, the long-term achievers obsess more about setting up specific ways to measure their progress.

Measuring What Matters and Keeping Score

Without feedback, you cannot adapt or improve. Measurement provides that feedback. And every time you get more information about how to do better, you are making a deposit in your Personal Capital account. It's what Builders do.

So here's the problem: We love to keep score as long as we are winning! When we're not—well, we don't really want anyone to see the report card. Builders see it differently.

"On the first day I was CEO, I only had one slide on the board in front of the entire management team. And there was one number on the slide," said Robert Lane, who leads John Deere & Co., Inc. Some employees tell him they remember the number had something to do with financial or operating metrics, but it didn't. The number was 18,000, and it meant "that we were going to have 18,000 employees within six months having written objectives of how we were going to work together—aligned teamwork—all linked to our overarching goals."

That alignment of people and the measurements is key. "We spend a great deal of time and energy in setting the right goals and finding the right ways to measure them," Michael Dell said. Big or small, Dell scrutinizes relevant details of what they do like a crime scene investigation "to see what makes a difference to customers."

Dell pays close attention to the evidence and refuses to be misled by "the things that we think are great because people ought to like it." As we walked with Michael through the slippery Davos snow in hiking boots and business suits, Dell recalled his famous tale about a time when he, as a teen, struggled initially with his paper route. It was "going nowhere" as a money-making venture until he noticed that people tend to buy a lot of new things—like newspaper subscriptions—when they had major changes in their lives, like moving into a new community, changing homes, having kids, getting married, and so on.

This observation yielded a breakthrough idea—to focus on life events and changes among the customers he served.

This allowed him to track that data to fulfill their unique needs at various stages of their lives. This same early interest in mapping customer data would later give him insight into buying habits for his computer business. As a teen, it generated success that brought him $18,000—a better salary than his skeptical teacher—and enough money to buy a BMW in high school when his peers were still asking for allowance money.

When Bad Goals Happen to Good People

Measuring things helps you take account of progress on your long hike toward your goal, but it won't tell you if you're headed in the right direction. It's important to start with the End in Mind, but it could be a dead end if you're in such a hurry to set a goal for yourself or for the sake of others without checking in with the first part of this book: finding a meaningful passion in life.

The goal-setting process is both powerful and dangerous because it can make you effective at achieving objectives—to take the hill, as they say—without any assurance that it's the right mountain for you to climb. Goals have no intrinsic meaning unless you invest meaning there. Goals don't come with a built-in guarantee that you'll benefit by reaching them or enjoy the process of getting there, nor do they assure you're on the right track. Goals, by their nature, don't necessarily require focusing on inspiration as much as they do on perspiration and the sheer pragmatic effort of getting things done.

There seems to be some confusion about what Steven Covey was evangelizing when he said start all things with the "End in Mind."

The challenge is to know which end to keep in mind.

"It's not a goal or even a destination necessarily," Covey said, "It's a way of life" to which we should aspire. "Let's say you've just had a heart attack," a key metaphor that Covey uses in his book, *The 8th Habit*. "What goals would you set with that life-threatening priority overhanging your decision? What are the important things worth doing with the time you have left? Why do we wait until we're hurt or injured to make decisions with the same level of caring for our future?"

The Secret Life of Goals

It's important to curb the rational impulse to set goals too soon on your journey. Goals become a barrier to success and satisfaction when they're not really yours. This is what we call the *Secret Life of Goals*—when the milestones themselves take on a life of their own. Goals can dictate success for its own sake or by someone else's definition, not necessarily success that matters to you and the stakeholders you care about.

In the world of business, you may be tired of hearing about Jack Welch's 20-year record as CEO of General Electric. But there is one last thing you should know about a BHAG that was once credited for his lasting success that ended up taking on a secret life of its own. Business books like *Built to Last* and many others lauded Welch's relentlessly clear goal to be #1 or #2 in market share in every GE business. But after years of pounding away at this no-holds-barred, take-no-prisoners battle cry for market share leadership, Welch himself was the first to blow up the definition he had worked so hard to proselytize.

The change was provoked when a group of senior military officials was invited to GE's training center in Crotonville. GE has long been known for inviting people from all walks of life to parachute in and swap ideas and best practices. One colonel insisted GE's market share goal of being #1 or #2 in every business allowed the company to get off the hook too easily. Welch was shocked.

Anyone with a little creativity, the colonel explained, "could describe a market so narrowly that you could become number one," Welch said. If you want to be in first place, then just measure success "in terms of being the number-one producer of chairs with curved armrests. I suddenly could see how you could game that system," Welch acknowledged.

"That idea hit me straight between the eyes," he said. It undermined the purpose of the BHAG in the first place. He never expected that an idea as pivotal as this would come from someone outside the company, let alone outside the business world.

What is more surprising is that it actually happened at all. "Neutron Jack," as he was once called for his stubborn stance during massive layoffs, was willing to stop being Jack long enough to realize the hill he was charging up was no longer the hill that needed taking. He stopped being the commander and chief for a moment and stepped to one side, looked over, and saw himself as a boss going in the wrong direction. He did not fall for a classic case of the *Secret Life of Goals* hijacking the real mission. It was serendipitous that the "Cavalry" arrived in the knick of time to deliver that surprising message AND that Welch was ready and able to hear the overall meaning of the mission—which for GE was growth, not just share.

Andy Grove had a similar epiphany. The former CEO of the world's largest chip company, Intel Corporation, is also known for his relentless clarity and disarmingly penetrating questions. He has been on well over a dozen business magazine covers unapologetically heralding Grove as one of the best business leaders in human history. When PBS' *Nightly Business Report* asked Wharton judges to vote on their top pick among CEOs of all time, they chose Grove. [7]

During one particularly difficult crossroad for Intel, Andy Grove and Gordon Moore, once CEO of Intel and creator of Moore's law, were sitting in a cubicle pondering the future of the business. (Yes, it's a tradition for even the boss to have a cubicle at Intel.)

What if things continued to get much worse and the board got rid of him? Grove speculated. Moore said the board would undoubtedly bring a new person in who would have courage as an outsider to do what few CEOs who are set in their jobs would be willing to do: Dump the core business. For Intel, this was memory chips. An outsider could come to the rescue to do something that dramatic, but not an insider who had put his career and ego on the line to stay bravely on the original course.

Grove had been raised in socialist Hungary, where he had resented a system in which the communist party bosses were never questioned and therefore innovation was impossible. His Jewish family had fled the Nazis during WWII, and he had changed his name four times, first to hide it and then to make it possible to pronounce. He had reinvented his life as an engineer in America with big dreams that he brought to Silicon Valley. Grove and his team sucked up the courage to drag themselves in front of the board with a preposterous idea that reinvented and, in retrospect, saved the company. He did radical surgery on himself, no matter how painful that was, exorcizing plans to hold onto Intel's largest business before it imploded on them.

Did they get lucky? Maybe. Did they earn it? Absolutely. The life of Andy Grove mirrors the meaning of the tale of the Princes of Serendip. Luck favors the prepared.

Keeping Your Goals Honest

Serendipity comes to those who do their homework and have the courage to do reality checks to determine whether or not they are still on course to achieve what actually matters about their goals. That brutal objectivity delivered the renewed growth that saved Intel.

By using meaning as their guide, Builders like Grove keep their goals honest. Not surprisingly, when the BHAGs embody what really matters, Builders find themselves well prepared to seize the best opportunities that serendipity can provide. Like the three princes, their successful journey is neither luck nor predetermined destiny. By living their values and paying attention, they are able to turn a steady stream of inevitable, unpredictable, and challenging events, in life and work, into good fortune.

CHAPTER 10

Naked Conversations—
Harvesting Contention

Disagreement is refreshing when two men lovingly desire to compare their views to find out truth. Controversy is wretched when it is only an attempt to prove another wrong.
—Frederick William Robertson

"I don't know if I would ever let anybody in there; they would probably be appalled," said Warren Staley. Outsiders aren't invited to his staff meetings, but insiders look forward to them. "I mean, there's emotion in terms of passion about ideas and debate."

Staley is chairman and CEO of Cargill, one of the world's largest private companies. With revenues of more than $70 billion, it is bigger than Dell, Microsoft, or Procter & Gamble, and—if it were a publicly traded company—it would have ranked in the top 20 on the 2006 Fortune 500 list.

"If you are lucky enough to recruit people who are as crazy and passionate about creating something great as you are, there is going to be contention," Staley insisted. "That's a given. We have really smart people from around the world running dozens of businesses. We come from different backgrounds, different cultures, but great experiences; and I say, that is the best thing that the company could have—a diversity of ideas and people challenging the heck out of others. I put myself up for that and I'm very comfortable doing that."

Contention as a Perk

It might not sound intuitive, but the best thing you can do about contention is throw fuel on the flames. You heard it right. One of the oddly inspiring ActionStyles of enduringly successful people is that contention is something they actually seek out. We're talking here about gloves-off, brutally frank dialog. It's what some pundits call *naked conversations*.

> *One of the oddly inspiring ActionStyles of enduringly successful people is that contention is something they actually seek out.*

Many entrepreneurs light up when you raise the topic. It's something they look forward to, and many said their team saw contentious meetings as a "perk" for working with them.

If this sounds like an episode of *Jerry Springer*, it isn't. Here's the difference: These naked conversations are not intended to be personally abusive (although you still may need a thick skin). The focus is on issues, not people. What Builders ignite is actually a sort of controlled burn where you set the fire with a match in one hand and hold a hose in the other. The purpose is to encourage contention in a very precise way to draw out the best, most passionate, and creative ideas from their teams.

Why is this so important? Former Chairman and CEO Mike McGavick of Safeco presided over the insurance giant's recovery from a near-billion-dollar loss when he took the role in 2001 to posting record earnings for the company a few years later. McGavick thinks creative contention is necessary insurance against corporate politics that often cripple productivity and growth.

"In the old Safeco [culture], I think it's fair to say that people kind of kissed up and kicked down. What you were told to do by your boss, you did without daring to question it," McGavick said. "And if someone were to say 'I don't think so,' that was an act of disrespect." While orchestrating the turnaround, McGavick wanted "everybody who has an opinion to voice that opinion and be involved in discussion. We then want to come to agreement, conclude and move on, and act with discipline. And getting to the right balance there is [hard] work. If people feel that words like 'collaboration' and 'alignment' are nothing more than new speak for the old system of 'do what your boss tells you,' then you've really lost a lot of corporate value because, of course, the aggregate corporate value—in addition to our financial balance sheet—is the collective intelligence of the people we're paying to come to work. And when they don't use that intelligence to its fullest, we are squandering a corporate resource." Without providing the opportunity for people to offer their creative input, you're wasting their brains and talent.

Struggle with the Issue, Not Each Other

Builders don't fend off contention; they manage it as a source of inspiration. If you can foster a safe place to air the issues, you constructively unleash power that will otherwise inevitably become toxic—festering and infecting things later. If the team keeps the contention around the issues, Builders welcome it. If folks begin to attack other people, the contention is not acceptable.

Gloria Fox, a committee member for the National Black Caucus of State Legislators, has dealt with contention on an almost daily basis since she took office as a Massachusetts state representative in 1985. "Politics is very personal. 'What is in it for me?' is how most people feel about politics. 'What have you done for me lately?' is what most people feel about politics. And then you have to take it another step forward—'What have *you* done?'" she said. You can start to shift selfish negative contention into positive energy, Fox advised, by giving people a constructive outlet. "You give people a task," she said. "You give people a job to do. Many people complain, but they definitely need to get busy on some form of action."

Contention about the issues, if left untapped and without an outlet, will become destructive down the road where it will be unwelcome, personal, and counterproductive. Worse yet, avoiding contention cheats you out of the best opportunity to unlock the most powerful ideas. This is fertile ground at the beginning of every project and a dustbowl if it never gets planted.

The essential key is Builders make sure the struggle is focused on creating something new or fixing the problem, not each other. We call it *creative contention*, and Builders find it to be a very good thing.

As an innovator at MIT for decades, until his death in 2001, Michael Dertouzos brought a sense of humanity to the technology world. But he said rarely did a week go by without a major wrestling match with his colleagues.

"I think dissent is very important, especially when it is toward a broad common goal. You agree on the broad goal and then you disagree and you quibble about how exactly to get there. All of us kind of fight with each other and I think if any one of us was missing, it would be a less powerful combination. It is important to let the differences and the tensions grow," he advised. "They contribute to changes that are very, very important."

Avoiding Delusions of Grandeur

In addition, creative contention can help your team avoid its own delusions of grandeur and dangerous self-agreement.

"When I ran a $2 billion division of Honeywell, I saw how you could stifle debate just as easily as you could encourage it. I found groups there where the lack of debate was just deafening," said former CEO Bill George, who is also author of bestselling *Authentic Leadership*. "In the beginning, people around there with strongly held views were labeled as prima donnas—sometimes their point of view was right and sometimes they were wrong, but you still needed their ideas and insights. Believe me, companies who don't value it miss out because the alternatives go unexplored, and some of those alternatives wind up being chosen paths."

George said his "ego and desires to be CEO occasionally got in the way while I was at Honeywell. I had 20,000 people working for me and I really wasn't strongly emotionally connected with the defense business as an industry." But when George landed the top job at Medtronic, a medical device creator and distributor, his heart was captured like no senior role had ever captured it before.

"I felt a switch turned on and I got engaged in ways I hadn't in my entire career." Instead of staying cozy in the corner suite at headquarters, he devoted much of his time in the field with the research physicians, sales team, and customers. He dressed in greens and peered over brain, heart, and spinal surgeries where doctors used his company's products, personally witnessing more than 1,000 medical procedures.

"It's okay not to find the right fit in your profession right away, but you have to keep trying and never settle. When you find the right fit, everything changes. And one of those things that change is the way you gain the confidence to really jumpstart the people around you. If you and your team are passionate and really believe in the cause, then you can't help but have fireworks. It was the culture at Medtronic. If what you're doing doesn't turn you on, and if you're holding back what you have to say or contribute, that is not okay. You're not going to be willing to hear the bad news or the best ideas. You're not going to be successful."

Ground Rules for Creative Contention

As candy king William Wrigley once said, "When two men in business always agree, one of them is unnecessary." Builders make contention not only acceptable, but required in a frequently held organizational gathering. One of the keys to making this debate a healthy one is a clear set of ground rules.

Staley recalled, "When I took over as CEO of Cargill, I wanted to define for the corporation a set of behaviors—to counter some very bad cultural habits we had gotten into. We got into a culture [where] you discussed, you made a decision, but you didn't agree with it, [so] you wanted to let everybody know, 'I didn't agree with this decision,' and you did everything you could to make sure it wasn't successful. I tolerated that sometimes, so we would go back and spend a lot of time rediscussing, redeciding with other people how we made that decision. I hated that. I was involved in that several times. I said, 'If I ever have enough say around here, enough authority, we're going to stop this,' because it's just really a cancer."

"So we said, 'Discuss, Decide, Support,' and when we walk out [of a meeting] we've made decisions we're all going to support diligently. It's okay to come back and say, 'It's not working;' we'll go back, we'll change it, we'll tweak it, we'll make a major change. But we will spend our energy trying to make this work," Staley said.

"We have all had to learn to practice behaviors and say, 'No, it is not your turn to talk, Freddie, you're listening right now,'" Staley laughed. At his meetings, "we all get poked in the ribs," he said. "You have to be pretty thick skinned. But I think, at a minimum, I promise our employees that we get at least 95% of the ideas out on the table. Now, you may not agree with our decision, but I can assure you, we've pretty well thought it through. If people think you are well intended, they give you quite a bit of latitude and quite a bit of respect."

Contention doesn't become evil unless you ignore it. Builders see creative contention as part of a rich collaborative process that never ends—it inspires action day in and day out in an ever-changing environment.

"You have to have a sense of humor in a company like this," Staley said. "We're in 60 countries where we're on the ground, and we're parading in and out of probably another 100 [countries where Cargill does business]. Every day, there's something going wrong. With BSE [Mad Cow Disease discovered in beef] two days before Christmas, we have a saying around here: 'If we ever click on all cylinders, we probably couldn't stand it.' It's never going to happen!" Managing a company of enormous global scope and complexity, Cargill uses creative contention to tackle inevitable daily challenges and get better at what they do every day.

> *Builders see creative contention as part of a rich collaborative process that never ends—it inspires action day in and day out in an ever-changing environment.*

Creating a Safe Time and Place for Contention

Many companies hold "workout" sessions where it's required to get all the issues out on the table.[1] When people really commit themselves to frank discussion, these meetings can be an effective way to create an appropriate politically correct environment to do what's usually politically incorrect at work. In other words, these meetings can be used to shift the focus from personality conflicts to the actual problems that need to be solved by providing a safer, more honest dialog without as much whining and name-calling. It provides a place to share the facts behind your worst fears and greatest hopes, rather than allowing them to continue to collide by accident.

The sooner you can do this, the better. Encouraging contention in the early stages of an initiative helps you discover where the problems are and fix them while they are small. Without a forum or time and place to attack and resolve the issues, relatively small problems can become counterproductive obsessions.

But, creating a time and place for contention just doesn't mean having lots of meetings. Vernon Hill, CEO and founder of rapidly growing Commerce Bank, gives his team members contentious 'panic buttons' that they can hit at any time to improve the business. "We have a policy of no stupid rules. We have an active policy in-house to pay people to give us stupid rules to kill," he said, pounding his fist on the table with a smile. "Fifty bucks to kill a stupid rule. Every computer in this company has a stupid-rule button on it. Any one of the team members can click on the button and give us a stupid rule to kill." This policy creatively challenges Commerce Bank employees to make things better for customers and the company in a very empowering way.

> *"Any one of the team members can click on the button and give us a stupid rule to kill."*

Creative Contention Is an Art that Builders Master

You might think that a concert orchestra would be another example of a place where this kind of highly empowered, creative contention would be a high art. Indeed, the metaphor of a symphony led by a passionate director is a favorite cliché used in leadership training. The irony is that even some conductors will be the first to admit they are among the worst examples of a dictatorship, with players seething in silent resentment.

"An orchestra player is about the least empowered human being on the planet," said Benjamin Zander, conductor of the Boston Philharmonic. "In fact, in a study they did at Harvard University of the various professions, they discovered that the orchestra player came in just below prison guards in terms of job satisfaction, which is a sort of tragic observation. The reason is that they have no voice, they have no say in the matter."

Zander had an epiphany when he turned 45. He realized that "the conductor of the orchestra is the only musician who doesn't make a sound," he laughed. "The meaning of 'symphonia' is 'voices sounding together.' So the job of the conductor is to make sure every voice is heard. Not only heard, but beautifully expressed. Because it is very easy to tell people 'you shut up, and you shut up, and you shut up and then this person will be heard,' but that is not what music is about at all. It's about getting people to be fully expressed—passionately engaged, giving their all—and still enabling everybody else to be heard, too."

"So I did something radical," he said, looking mischievous. He "put this white sheet [of paper] out on the stand of every musician and, of course, at first most of them ignore it. Some don't write anything, but many do. I read every single one of them. I encourage them to speak out. In fact, some people come into my rehearsals and say, 'My God, it is like a Quaker meeting house here.' I mean here is a pile of 35 of these white sheets and each one of them has something to say. Now, it may be a practical thing like 'What did the composer mean at this moment?' or 'We seem to have a difference of opinion between the trumpets and the oboes about the articulation of this phrase.' Those are very practical things and we can settle those and it is a good way of communicating because an orchestra player cannot speak to a conductor."

Lack of open contention breeds cynicism, Zander insists. People will act as though they don't "want to get involved in something that is going to end up in another disappointment. But if you keep talking to the passion, keep talking to the passion, keep talking to the passion, you will find that the cynics disappear. They aren't there anymore because a cynic is just somebody protecting themselves against more disappointment."

As people fail to have naked conversations, creative ideas become secret assets hoarded by team members rather than a shared resource making the team stronger. "It's not my idea or your idea; it's our idea," Zander said. "Often, we treat all the people who could help us achieve our goals as competitors and get into a zero-sum-game survival mode."

Whenever the team starts to see their interactions with each other as a matter of winning and losing points against each other, it spells disaster over the long haul, Zander cautioned. "You are either up or you're down, and you're worrying and you're looking and you're comparing and you're maneuvering and you're strategizing and trying to get people out of the way and getting a leg up on the next person. That entire whole neurotic world of 'Am I good enough? Are they better?' is all under the downward spiral thing. Most of us live most of our lives there. But vision doesn't live there. Vision essentially lives in contribution to humanity. I mean it sounds very grand. But that's what it is."

Attention, Intention, and Contention

Builders put their attention on making a contribution by doing something that also contributes to their own passionate soul. That's their intention. It's also the genius of the AND. When you focus your attention, keeping your thought and action aligned with meaning and staying clear about the intention, you can harvest contention. Passion is tense, by definition, just as pain and anger are, Alex von Bidder told us. He owns the Four Seasons Restaurant in

New York, where many people claim there is more power in the room at noon than in the West Wing of the White House. In addition to running his business, von Bidder travels the nation and the world leading men's therapy and spiritual development groups.

"When you join the tension (that's the definition of *contention*—meaning "with tension"), then you can put contention to work for you right away before it works you over later."

Candice Carpenter, founder of iVillage, agreed. "I always promoted an environment in which the exchanges were extraordinarily open and debate was highly favored," she said. "The way I did that was by letting people debate ferociously with me as CEO. And so, people saw that everyone still got promoted, everyone still got all of the rewards—even if they told me they thought my idea was really stupid. And, that has a very freeing effect on an organization when people feel that while you respect everybody for their intellectual position, the intellectual exchange is without boundaries. You have to be able to take it, but it is worth it to see everybody kind of intellectually turned on, which they will be in that kind of environment."

You Walk in the Door and the Best Idea Wins

Carpenter loved one particular meeting where the brainstorming sounded like ice hockey. "We had a meeting, which had directors, vice presidents, senior vice presidents, and I was always there. And it was standing room only. No one ever missed this meeting. I had people begging me to get into this meeting in a world in which people had too many meetings. It was a strategic meeting, and the rule was, you walk in the door and the best idea wins. People loved this meeting, and the quality of work from the most junior people in that meeting was—I have never seen anything like it—because they knew that if their idea won and they had their argument together, and had done their homework, they would have direct influence on the direction the company went. It was very exciting."

Not everyone on her senior team was crazy about contention. "Now, I did have people afraid of that in my senior team. I had some people feeling that we had the French revolution or something. It did scare some people who came out of very old-school companies. It scared them to death because it was like the inmates had been given the keys. But, I thought the results spoke for themselves. I mean, a lot of times, what happens is that the real intelligence percolating in the organization gets directly to the top. It doesn't have to go through eight filters and get watered down. You get the insight in its pure form."

Don't Be Right, Be Effective

In the final analysis, the point in all this is to be effective. Long-lasting achievers do feel zealous about the overarching goal they have set for themselves. But what really surprised us—over and over again—is how their obsession to reach their goal didn't prevent them from hearing and harvesting many different ideas about how to reach that outcome. That's where the struggle is focused.

Greg Foster, chairman and president of filmed entertainment at IMAX, thinks this is what differentiates the average movie director from those who have potential for greatness. No matter how dogmatic a movie director is about his or her project from a creative standpoint, a director with great potential is extremely effective at capturing insights from other people and fueling creative contention, he said. "They listen. A lot of young directors love to hear themselves speak. The ones who aren't afraid to ask for help and say, hey, I've got a really strong point of view on this, but there are some things I don't know and I could really use your help. Those are the ones that you know are going to make it."

Other people's assertions are judgments based on experiences seen through the lens of their values and ThoughtStyles at one particular moment in time. Their perspectives may be more effective in reaching your ultimate goal right now or yours may be, but chances are that the combination of different views will more likely be the perfect alchemy to help you get where you would like to go over the long term. It's the genius of the AND, not the tyranny of the OR.

"Normally, what people are trained to do is to be right and if possible to make the other person wrong," conductor Ben Zander sighed. "When you raise your finger up and point at them, saying you 'need to, you ought, you should, you must,' it closes down every imaginative bone in the body." When you have to be right with your team, it's like pulling the plug: You can see the light in everyone's eyes go dark.

"When you feel that you're making a contribution, that's when you get the shining eyes—when we get up in the morning and we live that," Zander added.

"It's all about shining eyes."

CHAPTER 11

Creating Alignment—The Environment Always Wins

Security is mostly a superstition. It does not exist in nature, nor do the children of men as a whole experience it. Avoiding danger is no safer in the long run than outright exposure. Life is either a daring adventure or nothing.
—Helen Keller

The 1967 riots left metropolitan Detroit, like many urban American cities, sharply divided along racial lines. Watching the violence on TV in the comfort of her suburban home, a young white homemaker became so outraged she abandoned her middle-class white neighborhood and moved with her husband and her five kids to the demographically black downtown shortly after the riots ended. Her sudden change of lifestyle was unwelcome in her family. Eleanor Josaitis was disowned by her father-in-law and was asked to change her name by her brother-in-law. When word got out that she was bent on bringing blacks and whites together, she endured hate mail and firebombs.

"There were moments when we were terrified," she sighed. "But that didn't change what we had to do." The people who showed up to help were recruited by Josaitis as volunteers for her nonprofit organization, "Focus: HOPE," which today provides food to 43,000 seniors, mothers, and children each month; career training programs in machining, engineering, and information technologies; child care; business conference facilities; community arts projects; and other outreach initiatives. Focus: HOPE has 400 team members and 51,000 supporters.[1] That's what is possible when you align a whole community—young, old, black, and white.

"Anything worth doing can't be done alone," Josaitis said. "There's been too much hero worship about how just one person does it all. At one point, we craved charismatic leaders, but that has been pretty well discredited, as we've seen smooth operators go to jail or fall way short of over-hyped expectations. Well, you CAN make a difference in a business or your community, but not if it's just about you. It's about finding other people who get inspired by their own belief that they can make a difference in a similar way—you've got to find other leaders who can make it happen with you!"

> *"Anything worth doing can't be done alone."*

"It is all about alignment between what you are and what you do—about making that fit together," Josaitis said, pounding her fist into her hand. There's always a little righteousness seeping from every one of her sentences. "You've got to recruit yourself to something you believe in, and then you have to recruit yourself to the right job—then go out there and seize the opportunity. And if you need a leader, you've got to recruit that person, too. It's about lining yourself up with a role where you feel as connected with the other people as you feel with the cause. When you feel that way, you've got a team."

Recruiting people to her team, she says, is about discovering "people whose dreams are like yours—and then not letting a single one of those folks get out of your sight or off the hook without doing something about it!"

Builders are people who, at some point in their life, got over the syndrome of thinking "we're all in this alone!"

Senator John McCain learned this lesson the hard way.

"Well, when I was a young pilot, I believed that all glory was self-glory. I believed that I needed no one, that I was perfectly capable of doing whatever I needed to do by myself. And I learned in prison that I was reliant and dependent on others, both for my physical well being, and then for my mental well-being. When I failed, they would pick me up, encourage me, and help me to go back into the fray again. The great privilege of my life was to serve in the company of heroes, a place where I observed a thousand acts of courage, compassion, and love."

Amazingly, McCain, who survived 5–1/2 years as a prisoner of war, described his brutal experience as transforming. He said he was grateful to Vietnam for strengthening his self-confidence and learning to trust his own judgment and that he didn't have to give up his sense of self to feel connected to other people.

"There is no greater feeling in life—no greater freedom— than to know that you can be yourself and part of a group that is engaged in a cause that is greater than you are," said McCain.

> *"There is no greater feeling in life—no greater freedom—than to know that you can be yourself and part of a group that is engaged in a cause that is greater than you are."*

Recruiting a Team in Support of Your Dream

Builders have this odd notion that many of the people they meet are a potential member of their community or team— as a recruit, a customer, a vendor, a volunteer, a friend, you name it. Even ex-employees qualify because they could take one of those roles in their next job. Here's where we are going with this: Would your behavior in working with others change if you knew in advance that your relationships would be long lasting? How would you build relationships if everyone you worked with, bought from, or served would always be your neighbor—or at least the smart, talented people you want to keep around?

You can't hide in a global virtual world. You'll likely run into the same folks regardless of whether you've intended for the relationship to be short or lasting, good or bad. It can be life changing to embrace this reality—think about everyone as a potential long-term member of your dream team.

Relationships Built to Last

If you want success that lasts, then you're better off if you think about your relationships as being built to last with people whose roles change—sometimes they work for you, sometimes you work for them, sometimes they leave your organization and become customers or your vendors or your regulators or your competitors. But, if you consider them on your virtual "team," the only thing that changes is their role. You still have the relationship.

Of course, you can't win them all. You won't be able to—or even want to—keep everyone on your team. However, as you watch how high achievers with long careers behave, and how their network of people grows richer and deeper over the years, it's obvious that most of them cherish their relationships. They keep high performers on their team—wherever those people may go.

If you've shifted your view that roles—employee, volunteer, partner, customer, vendor, neighbor—may change over time, but your network or team doesn't, then you're thinking long term and you'll set yourself up for relationships

that are built to last. And when you believe that you're relationships will be lasting, you'll behave in ways that treasure
relationships.

You're Only as Good as Your People and Other Tired Clichés

Builders spend what feels like an excessive amount of time
talking about the need to recruit and care for talented people to support the dream. Napoleon Hill[2] famously advised
fans to create a mastermind group—a sort of personal
board of directors who share common interests and ambitions, whether it was for their local PTA, a church, or for
the management of a major corporation.

The Builders we interviewed talked about this as if it was
big news, and most wished they had learned this earlier in
school or their careers. They went to great lengths to say,
over and over again, that they spent the largest percentage
of their time tracking down, surrounding themselves with,
and developing the people they variously described as "A"
players, top talent, leaders, enablers, great managers, Level
5 executives, angels, saints—all credited as the people who
supported the dream or actually did the work. We could
hardly get Builders to stop uttering superlatives about their
people.

The reason this feels like a cliché is because it is. If
you've ever listened to a CEO speak at the annual meeting
or read an annual report, you'll never escape without a bro-
mide about how employees are the greatest asset.

Don't Believe in Words—Only Believe in Behaviors

Indeed, most everybody gives it lip service, but this doesn't
mean it isn't true. One way you can tell whether you're

witnessing the real deal is to apply the *Porras Principle*: "Don't believe in words—only believe in behaviors." Watch the behavior of long-lasting high achievers and you'll see the difference. The walk matches the talk. People judge your values and character based on the difference between your words and actions. Everyone is better off when deeds and testimony match. Although political expediency can be tempting, Builders find that when their core values, words, and actions are in alignment, they feel like they're on track and, not surprisingly, they attract the right people to their team.

Senator John McCain, with quiet transparency, related a painful lesson about being expedient instead of maintaining alignment of his values, words, and behavior.

"You can do things that appear beneficial and may give you temporary advancement or movement along your path, but unless it's something you really believe in, it's not going to, in the long run, succeed. Every time in my career that I've done something for political expediency, I've later regretted it. When I've taken on an issue, even if it's unpopular at the time to take the position that I've taken, always at the end of the day, it's turned out right," he insisted.

"I'll give you a small example. When I ran for president of the United States, the confederate flag issue in South Carolina was a big issue. It was flying over the state capitol in South Carolina. Because I thought that it would gain me votes, I said, 'It's a state issue. It's not my issue,' which was clearly a cowardly approach to the issue—I still lost and, at the same time, displayed cowardice. I went down afterwards and apologized but that didn't mean anything. At the time that it was important, I took the political route rather than the route that I knew was correct."

There is a higher road for you to take, McCain advised: Stick with what you know is right. Period. And when you don't know something, he said, just say so. In fact, when Builders are asked a question for which they have no answer, most will say something almost never heard on prime time television (maybe the FCC has actually banned the words). It is perhaps the most provocative and courageous phrase anyone can say in public. In fact, the Dalai Lama, the global spiritual leader of Tibetan Buddhism, who is spending his lifetime trying to build understanding among faiths around the world, has been caught unabashedly using the phrase, in public, in at least five metropolitan cities just this past year. He says, with a smile and without apology: "I don't know," when asked a question for which he has no answer.

Nervous laughter will usually creep over the audience; then they sit in stunned silence as he grins on stage like a bald leprechaun in orange robes and sneakers. Seems shockingly simple in a world where so-called experts speculate on national television far beyond their training or expertise—shouting at each other about things they do not know.

Although it may not initially sound reassuring, "I don't know" is a sort of a code or catch phrase you can use to identify honest people and enduringly high achievers all over the world. It's kind of the secret handshake of integrity. When asked a question for which you do not have an answer, spend a moment looking earnest, then as folks lean forward breathlessly to await your wisdom, say "I don't know." It works wonders and creates a space in which learning is possible.

Many Builders as individuals have world-class minds, but actually know little or nothing about most things. You can be excused for nodding off at points during the last 200 pages, but if you take anything away from this diatribe, it should be this: The thing that matters is meaning! It drives everything. Builders align their attention to the things that matter to them, and they know a lot about that stuff. They are experts on what matters to them—their portfolio of passions. They talk responsibly in the domains of their

> *The thing that matters is meaning! It drives everything. Builders align their attention to the things that matter to them, and they know a lot about that stuff.*

expertise; otherwise, they say "I don't know."

The Dalai Lama cares about many things, but he doesn't have all the answers. Like other great spiritual leaders, he knows some very important things with exquisite detail and depth. That is because Builders are disciplined junkies about context. They are fanatical about framing what they say in terms of their goals and values. Most questions they are asked end with a segue back to the goal or mission with which they are passionately engaged. It's like a broken record. Only seconds after saying, "I don't know," they tell you what they do know about their passion or goal. When folks mess up, they talk about how that behavior didn't support the goal. When members of their team excel, Builders talk about how that work supported the goal or values. They work hard to avoid getting off the point.

The idea here is that human beings are fundamentally linguistic beings and act through language. Builders use language to create a shared sense of reality and to manage meaning for their partners and team members. Action is managed through language.

Intuitively, they are always pushing and shoving the three circles into alignment. Everything that has meaning gets organized in a ThoughtStyle, which then is turned into words and deeds—and ActionStyles—that support what matters to them. They use every opportunity to reaffirm goals and meaning.

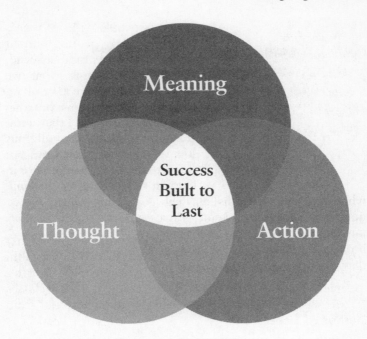

The Power of Language

"I watch my language because words hit people hard," Joe Nichols, Jr., cautioned. "When I catch myself saying the wrong thing or more often, when (his wife) Bonnie does, we try to get back on track. What you say really matters. Your words have to match where you're heading," he said. Joe is always watching whether his words and actions match his intentions, and are aligned with what he is trying to do. He might not feel strong or courageous today—in fact, "I often don't. But if I do those three things—if my words, action, and intentions match—without fail, it all works out."

Highly accomplished people use language in an instinctive or intuitive way—and it's focused on what they're trying to accomplish. Human beings use words to "get things done" or "mess things up," Joe said, so he pays close attention to how

Highly accomplished people use language in an instinctive or intuitive way—and it's focused on what they're trying to accomplish.

he treats people with his words and how he is treating himself with the chatter inside his head. If you're wondering what we mean by that, we're talking about the voice you just heard in your brain that asked that question. As you've noticed all your life, that voice in your head can be as toxic as it is supportive in helping you reach your goals.

But don't let it hijack or subtly and insidiously undermine your long-term objectives.

What you focus on in your words and actions impact your effectiveness and, as studies now confirm, your health. "Surprisingly, stress disability claims often increase after people take stress management workshops. Those classes can teach people to see more stress in their lives," said author Al Siebert. [3]

Your words and actions can make you feel better too, helping you manage your attitude and keep on track, not the other way around. Enduringly successful people the world over tell us it's no accident that, when you commit to progress with a strong narrative and matching deeds, you chip away and eventually overwhelm toxic thoughts and feelings.

"Sometimes, it feels as though you have to take back your feelings by force, like they've been kidnapped by a terrorist in your head," said leadership author, Terry Pearce. "But you can avoid the fight by neutralizing the enemy with words and actions that support your purpose—to rise above the fray."

When Builders pay close attention to what they say and do—and make sure both those things are focused on their long-term aspirations rather than the emotion of the moment, then they discover, miraculously, they've developed a better attitude! This in turn shapes their "ecosystem" for success.

The Environment Always Wins

"Play out your dream. There is no second chance. You either choose to impact your environment or your environment will define you," said Bill Strickland, CEO of Bidwell Training Center and the Manchester Craftsman's Guild. Strickland, who once chaired the Expansion Arts Panel for the National Endowment for the Arts, has used his lifelong passion for the arts to turn around the lives of thousands of people living in poverty.

"People who are poor can't ever imagine themselves in circumstances other than misery. If you build world-class architecture, and you open it up and you have lots of light and lots of ambiance, what happens is people feel more optimistic about life itself. By virtue of the fact that they are physically in this space, their temperament changes, their demeanor changes, their sense of themselves changes. And I believe that's the first step that's essential to the transformation of people who are fundamentally disadvantaged and who feel effectively left behind in life."

The physical environment is one important part of the whole "ecosystem" that supports the mission that you're committed to. On the basis that anything worth doing can't be done alone, your ecosystem includes your personal team, your organization, and where you spend your time. There are five major elements you can organize the environment around—there's the structure, culture, systems, technology, and physical setting. Success or failure in the long term will rely on how well aligned those things are with the incentives you've put in place and the behaviors you need for success—everything in that "ecosystem" can inspire or demotivate you and the team. It's not just one thing; it's everything working together.

No matter how skillfully you recruit the right people to your dream or organizational environment, you can't do a lot about what's inside another person's skin. We're talking here about an individual's own personal history and experiences: all his or her successes, and all his or her disappointments and demons. Some details of his or her life probably represent more information than you want to know anyway, but other parts are necessary to understand even if you can't change him or her. As former quarterback and pro football hall-of-famer Steve Young quipped, "Some people love to get yelled at. Others would be devastated if you yelled at them. And, you better know the difference."

We're all different inside; we all have different aspirations, motives, goals, perceptions, cultural influences, and so on. What you can have direct impact on is what's outside a person's skin. If you are the organizational leader, or even if this is just your department, then it's your job to think about the whole environment in which your team is attempting to work and succeed. When the environment—what's outside their skin—delivers confusing signals about what they ought to do, you get behavior that is all over the map.

Let's make this personal for a moment and place you in an organization in which the boss is asking for one thing, and you get paid by the organization to do something else, and your fellow teammates have yet another idea of what to do—which signal are you going to respond to? Well, a lot of that is rooted in who you are and what your history is.

If you have a very dominant father, for example, you might respond much more (or much less) to what the boss said. If you were a real social animal, you might respond more to what your coworkers said. If you were really ambitious and started selling newspapers when you were seven, you might respond more to what the reward system says. What you respond to is going to be different based on what's inside your skin. If the signals in the organization are aligned, then there is some predictability about how you will respond.

The basic model for success that lasts is built on knowing what behaviors you want from yourself, from your team, and in your organization, and aligning all the signals and incentives you're sending throughout the system, including to yourself. This is an easy thing to say, but it is very difficult for any individual or organization to do. Most people and organizations never achieve a high degree of alignment. We've all been in a place where we've tried to get things done despite the environment. It is possible for a while, but it's really hard work and rarely sustainable.

In Search of the Miraculous

Among the three of us, we (your authors) have worked with literally tens of thousands of people in our professional careers as executives, consultants, teachers, and coaches. We have witnessed individuals grow miraculously. According to the dictionary, a miracle is an event in reality beyond and out of the ordinary. Based on this definition, all the people we interviewed for this project have lead miraculous lives.

You can debate "is it genes or is it the environment," but why would you? You can't do anything about the former, and you can do a great deal about the latter. Science has even determined you can even do something about the nongenetic stuff that's inside your skin. You can have an extreme makeover and it does start inside your head, AND it requires what we'll call extreme environmental hygiene. What does that mean? Alignment. That requires that you get out of your life all the stuff that is inconsistent with your passions and goals. That includes people. Sounds harsh—can't help that—it is the way it is. You bring into your life everything that either supports or undermines who you are and what you want to create. Choose wisely. Of course, this is a process—not a light switch. It's tough and it can take awhile.

It's About Understanding Incentives

What's amazing to us is how enduringly successful people use infinitely different versions of this approach to build alignment—whether they're at home or in a Fortune 500 company that has hired the world's most expensive consultants or is using sophisticated software. Here's a simple, powerful practice that many Builders use.

Pick a behavior you don't like going on that you'd like to get rid of, but it just keeps showing up. Look at everything in the environment that rewards that behavior and all of the things that block that behavior. You'll find that the first list is a lot longer than the second list.

Then, pick a behavior that you'd like, something that's really important for success that isn't happening enough, and do the same analysis. You'll find that the list of things blocking those desired behaviors is a lot longer than the list driving progress.

It's about the payoffs, as Dr. Phil would say, that reinforce or sabotage behaviors and therefore make it easy or hard to achieve your goals and purpose. The trick is to get the messaging and incentives better aligned with the behaviors you really want. This is as true in your personal life as it is at work.

"Show me how a man plays golf and I'll tell you how he lives his life," says Fred Shoemaker, one of the greatest golf coaches practicing today. People tell him that they play golf for peace of mind—they like being relaxed, and the chance to be in nature with friends, to be themselves, and to let go. But when Shoemaker asks them what they want to get out of their golf workshop, "They say things like 'stop my slice,' 'fix my short game,' 'improve my score,' 'achieve more power,' and all the things that golfers want." Their first answer had to do with enjoyment, the second focused on what was wrong with their game. In golf, as in life, there is a problem when goals are not aligned with meaning. In golf, life, and business, too many people wait for satisfaction to come at some distant point in the future, when everything finally works. Ironically, "Without the joy, we can rarely have the stamina and passion to achieve things that we're after!" Shoemaker said. Your goals should give you some satisfaction from the moment that you set them in motion—that's one of the tests that let you know they are meaningful to you.

The Secret

We acknowledge that it takes tremendous commitment, discipline, and sometimes great courage to continuously engage in the practice of alignment.

The only thing that provides lasting success (and happiness, if that's part of your personal definition of success) is the day-by-day practice and struggle to move the three circles—Meaning, Thought, and Action—toward alignment in your life and work. It is an adventure that you are better off embracing with all of your heart and soul because it is a challenge that never ends as long as you are here.

So far, this has been quite a journey for us. We say "so far" because we have learned from Builders that lasting success requires lasting engagement, and there is so much yet to learn. Legendary television writer and producer Norman Lear said that one of his touchstones of success is to have served as a lightning rod for socially important dialogs. We hope this book serves as a lightning rod for a continuing dialog about success that serves us all. In the meantime, if there is such a thing as the secret we have found, this would be it: If you want *Success Built to Last*, then *Create a Life That Matters* (to you).

The Pleasure of Finding Things Out[†]— A Look at the Research Behind *Success Built to Last*

Background and Methodology

We have always been deeply moved in the presence of people who are great at what they do—people who have found a way to live their potential. Finding out about the lives of people who are able to do this has been one of the great pleasures of creating this book. Our conversations with remarkable people yielded an embarrassment of riches, and some process had to be devised to hone in on the key ideas and behaviors that enable these people to live as they do.

Sometimes, even very accomplished people cannot accurately articulate their own process—they simply do what they do—almost beyond the threshold of consciousness. We use the word *consciousness* here to mean "to be aware of what one is doing and why." In other words, many successful people are busily doing mostly what works without always being certain about what they are really doing and why.

Good research can solve much of the mystery in all of this. It's rather like playing Sherlock Holmes. As the mysteries are solved, excellent coaching becomes available that we

† Used with appreciation to Richard P. Feynman, et al.[1]

217

can all use to live closer to our full potential. Whatever we are, we can now learn to be a great one!

What follows is written for all of you who have a degree of curiosity about the ins and outs of this process. Some of the data are so compelling that we notice our own thinking about success and what it means to people has been changed for the better. We also notice that some of our behavior has changed, also for the better. You may find what follows has a similar impact on you.

> *What follows is written for all of you who have a degree of curiosity about the ins and outs of this process.*

If you have read *Built to Last*, you may recall that the research method used in that study was characterized by three key components:

1. **Sample selection**—750 CEOs were surveyed and asked to nominate up to five companies they considered to be the most "visionary." (This process ultimately yielded 18 companies that were included as visionary companies, along with 18 companies in a comparison group.) Two sources were used to select the CEOs surveyed.

   a. First, 500 CEOs were selected by taking a stratified sample from the two 1990 Fortune 500 lists of the largest industrial and service companies in the United States.

   b. Second, 250 CEOs were selected from the two *INC Magazine* lists of the fastest-growing private and public companies. The 18 most frequently nominated companies made up the visionary company sample set.

   c. **Age**—Additionally, selected companies had to be old enough to have had a minimum of two different chief executive officers. The two youngest companies in the final sample were founded in 1945.

2. **Historical perspective**—The entire life history of all the companies was studied based on data gathered from books, magazine and newspaper articles, Ph.D. dissertations, masters theses, and company archives.

3. **Comparison group**—For each visionary company, a comparison company was selected based on it being:

   a. Founded in approximately the same time period as the visionary company

   b. In the same industry

   c. Key competitor for the visionary company

   d. Seldom mentioned in the CEO survey described previously

   e. Still in business in 1990

For *Success Built to Last*, we conducted two extensive and entirely independent studies that together tested and compared insights into the traits of successful people. These two pieces of research differ substantially from the *Built to Last* research for many important reasons, not the least of which was that this book is focused on individuals in all walks of life, rather than being limited just to organizations listed on the stock exchanges. For more than a decade, leaders have been asking us to provide greater insights into the success and leadership of all types of organizations, and pursuing two new studies gave us the opportunity to employ the genius of the *AND* principle from *Built to Last*.

Exploratory Field Research

The first of the two *Success Built to Last* studies consisted of ten years of field research—a series of personal interviews with a remarkably diverse group of enduringly successful people. These meetings were conducted in some of the best places to observe actual behavior—in the homes and offices of these leaders and during their travels to communities and worksites. This approach allowed us to observe leaders in public companies, as well as those in nonprofit community organizations, government agencies, privately held small and large businesses, and solo practitioners (from schoolteachers and scientists to entertainers, athletes, and authors). The process provided a rich set of insights and hypotheses that we believe could not possibly have been derived in isolation, or by traditional survey methodologies. The second *Success Built to Last* study tested key findings of the first study in an independent, quantitatively based *World Success Survey*.

The first study employed the following methodology:

1. **Sample selection**—The people we were interested in interviewing were individuals whose traditional successes had lasted for decades, including many Nobel Laureates, government and community service leaders, teachers, scientists, and Olympians, as well as Pulitzer, Grammy, Peabody, and Academy Award winners and the CEOs of large and small organizations.

   a. To identify these people, we reviewed an eclectic variety of well-established lists—such as *Time Magazine*'s *Most Influential People*, as well as those on the annual honor rolls of the biggest, fastest-growing, or admired in major business publications, notably *Forbes* and *Fortune*. We also looked at lists of noteworthy individuals honored at nonprofit organizations, such as Oprah Winfrey's *Use Your Life Award* winners.

      i. We believe that lists of successful individuals drawn from magazines, newspapers, and other agencies are an appropriate surrogate for the CEO survey done in *Built to Last*.

   b. The individuals to be interviewed were screened to identify a diversity of interests, industries, and gender. Selected individuals were required to have a minimum of two decades of impact in one or many areas of endeavor. This 20-year minimum is parallel to the minimum age criteria established in *Built to Last* by requiring at least two generations of CEOs.

c. We invited several hundred people to participate and, ultimately, completed more than 200 personal interviews from 1996 to 2006.

2. **Historical perspective**—In preparation for each interview, we reviewed the relevant biographical information about each subject from books, magazine and newspaper articles, and organization websites and archives. Because it was not possible to determine conclusively how a person thought about his or her life from his or her earliest years to the present, using external resources, we decided to use as the source of information what individuals said about themselves and their perceptions of how they built their lives and careers over time.

a. Data were collected from the research subjects in unscripted, exploratory, wide-ranging interviews focusing on success and leadership in their lives and the principles that guided their careers. The key challenge was to tease out the core dynamics in the lives of these remarkable people. We believe we achieved the maximum rigor possible given the constraints of a study of highly impactful individuals. (In the end, you are the best judge of any results we report—does it make sense to you and could it be helpful?)

b. The contents of hundreds of fascinating personal interviews were analyzed and coded by organizational theme codes and behavioral points of view—based on the rich narratives that have been shared throughout this book. A more detailed description of the methodology and data analysis approach

used in this study is presented in later sections
(see Exhibit 1, "The Personal Interviews and
Other Data Analysis").

3. **Comparison group**—We recognized early in the
process of developing *Success Built to Last* that we
would need a way to test our conclusions with a comparison set, even though it is always difficult to estab-
lish a "control" group for a human population based
on the many competing definitions of success. Because
we were not studying public companies, we could not
use the same process as *Built to Last*.[2] Instead, we
believed it was useful to see whether our results
would be confirmed if we were to develop and admin-
ister an independent survey—the *World Success
Survey*—based on an unrelated sample of respondents, using a completely different method from the
personal interviews that we gathered over the past ten
years (see Exhibit 1). The results were remarkable,
adding incredible depth and insight into a decade of
field research in personal interviews.

The World Success Survey

With our manuscript already drafted, our Stanford-based
team partnered with our colleagues at Pearson/Prentice Hall,
The Wharton School at the University of Pennsylvania, and
the i-Novation division of Moskowitz Jacobs Inc. (MJI) to
develop and conduct a self-administered internet survey. The
poll, which we called the *World Success Survey*, was
designed with the objective of validating the findings captured in the authors' interviews with enduringly successful
people around the world. The factors and levels included
in the survey were derived from the authors' research as
reflected in the book.

In the spring of 2006, we communicated to readers of the Knowledge@Wharton about the opportunity to participate in a global study about success. Knowledge@Wharton is an online publication with a circulation to managers, educators, and other professionals at senior and junior levels in 100 countries. Readers of the online publication were invited to participate in a global survey on how people think about success (see Exhibit 2). Those interested in participating clicked on the designated link and were provided with brief instructions on how to participate in the survey (see Exhibit 3). During the first week, 365 people responded to the survey, and the results were embodied in this analysis.

Demographically, respondents were two-thirds male and one-third female, and the age splits were 23% under age 35, 57% 35-54, and 20% 55 and over. Altogether, 66% of the respondents were from the United States, with the remaining 34% distributed across the world—i.e., 13% from Asia, 9% from Europe, and 12% from other locations.

The survey used Dr. Howard Moskowitz's proprietary IdeaMap technology, a method that is used for consumer attitude studies. The theoretical foundation of Moskowitz Jacobs, Inc.'s (MJI) work is experimental design and mathematical modeling. The IdeaMap evolved from the method of conjoint analysis, and from an analysis of what Moskowitz calls, the "algebra of a person's mind." The IdeaMap survey format engages respondents in the "job" of reacting to a series of screens. The idea here is that even if a respondent is totally unable to articulate what he or she feels, nonetheless the results come bounding forth. Each screen displayed a "menu of success" incorporating unique combinations of 3–4 aspects or vignettes about "lasting success" based on narratives from our personal interviews—i.e., views about the definition of success or how people feel about failure, goal-setting, or assigning blame (see Exhibit 4).

Each respondent reacted to these success menus, developed via experimental design, using the rating scale of 1 (very poorly) to 9 (very well) to indicate how well each menu described "your view of lasting success." Moskowitz Jacobs Inc. had originally developed and validated the IdeaMap testing instrument in the late 1980s and 1990s to encourage intuitive responses and honest feedback rather than the "gaming" behavior that may be present in other, more pedantic, survey methods. In this way, the survey uncovers how people really feel about factors related to success.

Regression Analysis and Impact Scores

Regression analysis (see Exhibit 5, "The Regression Model,") relating the rating responses to the test stimuli (our "menus of success") show the contribution (positive or negative) for *each of the 36 aspects* of success (see Exhibit 6). These scores are the basis for measuring the absolute impact of each aspect of success and comparing that impact to all the others. The result is a wide range of scores across the 36 success aspects in this research, from a high of +21, indicating a very positive relation to success, to a low of -28, indicating a very negative relation. (Our experience suggests that, for this research, scores of +6 or higher and -6 or lower are identifying important and notable results.) Such a wide range of scores underscores the strongly-held feelings being expressed by the respondents, and allows us a clear reading of these feelings.

Respondents also answered questions on how successful they considered themselves to be both professionally and personally. These self-identifications are the basis for placing respondents in the successful/unsuccessful groups for analysis. Of the 365 people who participated in the survey:

- 35% identified themselves as successful both professionally and personally.

- 31% identified themselves as unsuccessful both professionally and personally.
- 23% identified themselves as only successful personally.
- 11% identified themselves as only successful professionally.

By analyzing the results for each group, we profiled the different sets of beliefs about what may contribute to being successful. We also compared the views of the "successful" people—the "S" group, as we will describe them here—versus those views held by the people who identified themselves as "unsuccessful" (the "U" group). The results from IdeaMap helped us understand what differentiates the minds of these two populations.

Finally, we examined key *demographic* categories—i.e., gender and age for insights into differences that might exist on how these groups view success and successful people (discussed in Section IV, "Selected Key Findings—Demographic Categories").

Overall Conclusions

This survey provided an independent and amazingly transparent source of comparison, supporting key findings from our personal interviews. Among the top line results were further confirmation that successful people don't rely on the approval of others to pursue their goals, causes, or callings. Successful people take the initiative *despite* social pressures rather than because of them. They are more committed to *doing* what they love than *being loved* by others. They don't wallow or obsess on a single defeat or rely on finding scapegoats or blame when things go wrong. Instead, successful people place higher priority on being effective in getting the outcomes they seek.

Regardless of whether the survey participants rated themselves as "successful" or "unsuccessful," all groups said that the traditional dictionary definition of success—notably the significant achievement of fame, wealth, and power—*no longer describes* what success means to them. Although popularity and affluence, for example, are nice outcomes, people prefer to define *success* as the ability to "make a difference," "create lasting impact," and being "engaged in a life of personal fulfillment," according to the study. What is special about enduringly successful people is that they won't settle for less than this!

As discussed in Chapter 7, "The *Tripping* Point: Always Make New Mistakes," and Chapter 8, "Wounds to Wisdom: Trusting Your Weakness and Using Your Core Incompetencies," Builders "harvest" their failures and successes as "data," which they then use to improve their effectiveness. Successful people also said that "loving what you do" is a *necessary* condition for success. Indeed, Chapter 2, "Love It or Lose—Passions and the Quest for Meaning," reviews the dangers of not doing what you love because people who have that passion can outlast and eventually outrun you in the task. In a global economy, for every person who is half-hearted in a job, there are dozens of others who are passionately waiting to take that job from them. Passion for what you do is not just a creative imperative—it is a competitive necessity.

The research study also provided a major breakthrough in our thinking regarding three *attitudinal* or *mind-set* segments. The response data from these key attitudinal groups provided further insight into our original interviews—revealing how different groups of people tend to behave. These mind-set groups are attracted to various dimensions of success. They are defined not by what they say about themselves, but their actual responses to the stimuli: what they think and how they define success. This is discussed in Section III, "Selected Key Findings: Attitude Segments—A Surprising Breakthrough."

Section I: Selected Key Findings: Successful People

The 35% of individuals in this survey who see themselves as being *successful both professionally and personally* express several very strong beliefs about what they associate with success.

Most importantly, this group believes being successful requires a commitment to make important things happen. Something must be created that makes a *difference*, and that something must have *lasting value*. They are not going to be satisfied with anything less.

Successful people strongly rate the idea:

- "Success means I can make a difference and create lasting impact" (+14).

The notion of happiness, however, gets only a modestly positive response compared with the other measures they use for success.

- "Success means I am happy" scores +6.

Successful individuals are more likely to define success in terms of personal fulfillment, and not by wealth or by social recognition:

- "Success means I am engaged in a life of personal fulfillment" scores a strong + 13, while
- "Success means I am achieving fame, money, or power" has a very negative -15 score among this group.

This belief in self-actualization is accompanied by a belief in self-reliance. These people have no interest in relying on others to tell them how to achieve what they want. They are not just doing it "for themselves," but they're also going to do it "their way":

- "To stay on track with my goals, it's best to rely on the opinions of others" is resoundingly rejected (-20 score).

Although personally focused on what they want to accomplish and how they want to go about accomplishing it, they are not a bunch of "loners." Quite the contrary, they understand the importance of contributing to and enjoying good relationships and being involved with others:

- "Success means I create strong relationships and connections with people" scores +9.

Being successful doesn't mean that these people haven't experienced failure. But, when they do, they use it as an important learning tool. In this way, they can better their odds of being successful in the future. They turn their wounds into wisdom:

- "I learn more from my failures than I learn from my successes" scores +7.

They understand their unique passions and allocate their view of the *right* amount of time to each (not equal or balanced portions, but rather their own individually chosen preference):

- "Balance to me is spending the RIGHT amounts of time on work, family, personal interests, and community" scores +10.
- "Balance to me is spending EQUAL amounts of time on work, family, personal interests, and community" scores –6.

They feel the freedom to choose what is important to do and act on it:

- "Success means I have the freedom to do what is meaningful" scores +9.

Setbacks do not cause them to give up on what they care most about:

- "Setbacks don't make me ABANDON my passions or causes" (+7).

They reject the idea that they must sacrifice something important to them to achieve another goal; they want both. As we learned in our personal interviews, enduringly successful people believe in the genius of the *AND* rather than the tyranny of the *OR*:

- "I prefer to pursue one of two alternatives rather than trying to make both work" scores a very negative −15.

Successful people also reject the idea that all their career steps have been planned out. They are more focused on what matters in their lives on each step in their journey, and make choices about what to do next based on what that action means to them rather than a preset plan. As noted in our personal interviews, they focus on those things that they care about, and when they do that, they are able to take advantage of the serendipitous opportunities that present themselves along the way rather than rely on a roadmap:

- "My career has followed a precise roadmap that I myself created" scores -16.
- "It's always been clear to me what I wanted to do for the rest of my life" scores -10.

This set of beliefs guides the actions of the S group. However, an examination of the beliefs of those individuals who view themselves as *both professionally and personally unsuccessful* (31% of respondents) shows a lot of similarities. So naturally the question becomes—what defines the *difference*? Although the U group wants to do meaningful things, the S group gives it a higher level of importance. It is *the priority* in the lives of successful people; whereas for people who say they are unsuccessful, it is more something that they would *like* to do:

- "The *main priority* in my life is to do meaningful things" scores a strong +14 among the S group versus +3 among the U group.

The S group is also uncompromising in its belief that "love" is a necessary requirement of their job, whereas the U group is relatively neutral about this need for loving their job:

- "It is absolutely necessary for me to work in a job that I really love" scores a +7 among the S group versus +1 among the U group.

In keeping with their beliefs of the importance of learning from failures and moving on, the S group is adamantly opposed to "playing the blame game," whereas the U group tells us that they have no strong views on this issue, or perhaps they have been the subject of that blame and therefore they see it as standard procedure!

- "I believe that when things go wrong, most people look for a scapegoat" scores -17 among the S group and -3 among the U group.

People who see themselves as unsuccessful are less secure about their work, feeling the need to appear "good" at everything they do. Successful people are more focused on what matters to them and are less concerned about how "good" they may seem to others along the way:

- "Whatever I'm doing, I make sure to be good at it" scores +10 among the U group and -2 among the S group.

Successful people don't obsess over what other people may think about their work. As was also revealed in our personal interviews, enduringly successful people are more concerned with *doing* what they love than *being loved*. They don't treat their passions like a trivial pursuit or low-priority item. Successful people focus on being good at what is meaningful to them, and do *that*, not "whatever" comes along.

People who described themselves as unsuccessful are also looking for (or feel that they have) acceptance among people who are significant in their lives, while the S group does not appear to worry much about that:

- "People who count support me in following my passions" scores +8 among the U group and zero among the S group.

As we learned in our personal interviews, enduringly successful people tend to do meaningful things because they matter, and they do these meaningful things *despite* popularity and social pressures.

Section II: Selected Key Findings: Professional Success Versus Personal Success

We analyzed the responses to all the 36 success aspects in the test, comparing the impacts by those who identified themselves as *successful professionally* compared to those who identified themselves as *successful personally*. We wanted to identify whether the notion of "success" was viewed differently in these two endeavors, and, if so, then in what ways?

The evidence in the research overwhelmingly identified that successful professional people held *the very same beliefs* about what contributes to their success as those people who were successful in their personal lives:

- Rating scores for each of the 36 aspects in this research showed no significant differences between people who identified themselves as *professionally successful* and those who identified themselves as *personally successful*.

These respondents believe there is "universality" to what makes lasting success in any endeavor.

Section III: Selected Key Findings: Attitude Segments—A Surprising Breakthrough

The IdeaMap technology we used for this survey analyzes the data to find key mind-set differences among the respondents and then segments those groups. People in the same mind-set segment "look the same" when we review which of our 36 specific factors drives them to describe success. *When we first looked at the mind-set segmentation, we did not recognize the power of what it was telling us.* Frankly, we were so fascinated that such an unrelated and independent research effort—the *World Success Survey*—had reaffirmed so many other aspects of what we had learned in our original interviews that we almost missed this additional dimension. We weren't sure we should even bother to include it in this discussion, but Moskowitz insisted that we take a closer look at it because the attitudinal segmentation was compelling and the statistical data were striving to tell us something significant about the specific mind-sets of these participants.

It was essential to compare what this scientific survey had discovered based solely on the mathematics of the IdeaMap algorithm with what we had gleaned, in more depth and richness, from our extensive personal interviews. The algorithm produced a set of results for each person in the study based on differences in the patterns of their responses to the stimuli. (No two respondents ever saw an identical order of the aspects of success on the survey because each person received a randomized set of elements!) People with similar patterns fell into the same mind-set segment, no matter who they were, or no matter how they described themselves. *This sophisticated statistical analysis revealed three distinct mind-sets in the survey, based solely on the way that the respondents in the survey reacted to the menus of success.* The segments were different, as you will see later. We were on to something—but what?

Looking deeper, our research director, Bonita Thompson, who possesses a remarkable gift for connecting the dots in enlightening ways, had yet another epiphany. She realized that what we were seeing objectively in the data emerging from the survey was the same three "Circles" of *Meaning*, *Thought*, and *Action* that we used to outline our methodology in the book! We were astonished that the IdeaMap survey had confirmed independently that there are, indeed, three distinctive attitudinal aspects of lasting success—meaning, thought, and action. In addition, the survey data had identified that there are notable attitudinal preferences that people have in this regard without realizing it themselves (nor did we at first!). It's not that these segments don't overlap on how to define success. It's just that, when push comes to shove, every individual tends to identify a bit more strongly with one of these three dimensions. The three dimensions are as follows:

- **Meaning**: The Make a Difference, Be Meaningful Segment (44% of sample).
- **ThoughtStyle**: The Allocating My Time to My Passions Segment (29% of sample).
- **ActionStyle**: The Be Accomplished and Love Work Segment (27% of sample). It's worth mentioning that there were no significant differences in these attitudes based on demographics. They were consistent regardless of age, gender, or geographic location.

Additionally, the likelihood of these groups to describe themselves as *being successful* was very similar across the three segments, as you see in the following table.

	Total Sample	Meaning Segment 1		ThoughtStyle Segment 2		ActionStyle Segment 3	
	N	N	%	N	%	N	%
Total Sample	365	160	44%	105	29%	99	27%
Successful professionally and personally	129	53	33%	39	37%	37	37%
Successful professionally but not personally	39	15	9%	12	11%	12	12%
Successful personally but not professionally	83	36	23%	24	23%	23	23%
Not successful in either	114	56	35%	30	29%	27	27%

Like all other segments of our sample, all three of the attitudinal segments—Meaning, Thought, and Action—agree about what success is

- "Success means I can make a difference and create lasting impact."

And, what it is not

- "Success (does not) mean I am achieving fame, money, or power."

However, the three segments differ quite distinctly, and occasionally dramatically, in some other belief areas.

Meaning

The largest attitude segment, containing 44% of the respondents, is the *Make a Difference, Be Meaningful* segment. This Meaning-oriented segment exhibits a somewhat lower likelihood of seeing themselves successful in both their professional and personal lives than does either of the other two attitude segments. (When it comes to "meaning," it's difficult to feel you're ever really finished or totally successful in all aspects of your life and work at all times. The key leadership task of managing meaning is never done, said Professor Warren Bennis, founding chairman of the Leadership Institute at the University of Southern California.)

The key distinguishing feature about this group is that they are even more strongly committed to making a difference/creating a lasting impact than are the other two segments. However, unlike the other two groups, this segment *requires* that everyone around them in their life and work share a common sense of meaning:

- "My boss supports what I believe to be meaningful and important" scores +9 versus -7 for the rest of the population (the other two attitudinal segments combined).

Another key feature that distinguishes this group is that their commitment to personal fulfillment is somewhat stronger:

- "Success means I am engaged in a life of personal fulfillment" (+12 versus +7 for the rest of the population).

ThoughtStyle

The second segment is identified as the *Allocating My Time to My Passions* segment, and it comprises 29% of respondents. The key distinguishing characteristic is a strong interest in recognizing what their true passions are and acting in a manner that addresses these various passions in the right proportion. They recognize their personal uniqueness, and are not simply reacting to society's expectations:

- "Balance to me is spending the RIGHT amounts of time on work, family, personal interests, and community" (a huge +21 versus +4 for the rest of the population).
- "Pursuing many different passions increases my effectiveness and creativity" (+12 versus +1 for the rest of the population).

Harvesting Contention

This ThoughtStyle-oriented segment, which represents almost a third of the sample, does not appreciate dissonance in their views from those of other people, whereas the other two attitudinal segments (the other two-thirds of the population) "harvest contention"—they readily embrace the inevitable creative arguments that arise when you are trying to build something meaningful:

- "It's essential to me to encourage people to share views that disagree with my own views." (The ThoughtStyle-oriented segment scores −8 versus a strong +12 score for the rest of the population.)

- "To accomplish what matters to me, it may be necessary to go against the wishes of people who count" (-11 versus +5 for the rest of the population).

Harvesting Failure

Although members of this ThoughtStyle-oriented segment don't like disagreements with others, they more readily embrace the learning that comes from setbacks. As enduringly successful people described in the interviews, they "harvest" failure:

- "I learn more from my failures than I learn from my successes" (+10 versus + 3 for the rest of the population). The Meaning-oriented group (the first attitudinal segment) scores +7, while the third segment (which we'll describe next) is an ActionStyle-oriented group that is less enthusiastic about harvesting failure (–3).

ActionStyle

The third attitudinal segment is identified as the *Be Accomplished and Love Work* group, and comprises 27% of the respondents. Above all else, this ActionStyle-oriented segment wants to love their job:

- "It is absolutely necessary for me to work in a job that I really love" (+15 versus -2 for the rest of the population).

And, they also want to see themselves as accomplished in it:

- "Regardless of what other people think, what motivates me most is doing a great job" scores highly (+12 versus +1 for the rest of the population).

Additionally, this segment loves to get things done and accomplish things for its own sake. They are very satisfied, never disappointed, with the goals they achieve:

- "Sometimes it's disappointing to achieve a goal and discover that it has little meaning to me" scores very low with this segment (-21 versus -2 for the rest of the population).

Alignment is essential: This IdeaMap research survey confirmed that people as individuals tend to resonate most strongly with one of the three circles (of meaning, thought, or action). Whereas many of us agonize over "balance" as society defines it, what is clear from this research study and our interviews is that the essential balance that we seek is likely to be an issue of *alignment* of the three circles—over what matters to us (meaning), how we think about those things and allocate our time to our passions (thought), and then how we proceed to get them done (action). The balance that we are seeking is to find our own personally defined portfolio of passions that we feel is *meaningful*— that fuel our creative *thoughts* and drive us to take *action* to manifest them.

Section IV: Selected Key Findings— Demographic Categories

Overall, there are differences in views about success across various age groups and among men and women who feel *successful both professionally and personally*. Females are somewhat more likely than males (40% versus 33%) to identify themselves as successful both professionally and personally. By age groups, the feeling of success increases with age—e.g., 59% among ages 55+ versus 20% for those under 45.

- Males and females agree that "Success means I can make a difference and create a lasting impact" is the most important aspect of lasting success (+12 and +16 respectively).

However, males also tend to associate success with doing a "great job" despite the opinions of the others:

- "Regardless of what other people think, what motivates me most is doing a great job" (+6 versus -1 for females).

Females tend to be more oriented to the importance of personal relationships and happiness:

- "Success means I create strong relationships and connections with people" (+11 versus +3 for males).
- "Success means that I am happy" (+9 versus +1 for males).

All age groups recognize the key aspect of success as "Success means I can make a difference and create a lasting impact," and they also exhibit similarities across a wide range of aspects of success.

However, the older respondents (55+) exhibit an even higher level of passion about this desire, with ratings above all other age groups:

- "The main priority in my life is to do meaningful things" (+14 versus +8 for the rest of the population).
- "It is painful to me not to do something that is meaningful" (+9 versus +1 for the rest of the population).

To draw any conclusions about differences in individual countries, our sample would need to be sliced up into pieces so small that they wouldn't be reliable. However, we did see enough variations in the data regionally to get us excited that there is more gold to be mined with further research. It will be well worth launching another more extensive survey nation by nation to uncover those insights.

This research identified a global view of "lasting success" in terms of what contributes to success and what it has come to mean for people. The traditional definition of success was resoundingly trounced in this survey, as well as in our personal interviews. It's amazing that society tolerates the old definition. It's clearly time to redefine the meaning of success in the dictionary, if not society as a whole. Please let us know about your definition of success, and make your views known to dictionary publishers. You can reach us at www.SuccessBuiltToLast.com.

Exhibit 1

The Personal Interviews and Other Data Analysis

Step 1: Exploratory Inquiry

What has been remarkable to us since we started this journey is that there are so few well-established, high visibility, or enduring inquiries into the meaning of success and leadership. We haven't seen major international campaigns underway to convince the dictionaries to change or expand the definition of success, for example, nor a major initiative to look at more meaningful and productive alternatives that might better serve organizations, business people, partners, parents, community leaders, or society as a whole. It is our hope and intention that efforts to better define success come flying out of the woodwork as this book goes into international distribution.

Indeed, we found in our live presentations that the combined topics of success and meaning discussed in the same conversation generate significant heat in the room—

as people struggle to rationalize preconceived or idealized notions (or personal demons) about what matters to them (as individuals and their organization) and what success should *really* mean.

The passion we felt also translated into considerable support for our exploratory approach to the eclectic collection of interviews that we have gathered along the way. Not only are people anxious to have this conversation, they are enthusiastic (or relieved) that we're taking a non-traditional approach to the subject. When we first reached out to the late Peter Drucker to conduct an interview with him for this project, we shared with him our interest in eventually developing a leadership survey in addition to our personal interviews. He admonished that "all that had been done before." He was not alone in his encouragement that we depart from pedantic methods—at least in the beginning of this journey—in two ways: A) To focus more on how leaders think about success than just leadership itself, and B) To approach this exercise as an open-ended exploratory set of interviews rather than a standardized test.

All three authors have coached, advised, and interviewed leaders for decades. The interviews upon which this book is based were initiated ten years ago as a practical business interest in capturing non-theoretical insights and practices for both individuals and organizations about success and leadership. We believe that real interviews with real people have great power to provoke richer discussion in the many contexts in which each of the coauthors has done their work: executive training programs, classroom sessions, publications, and also for public broadcasting programs and other consulting venues.

Over the years, we have taken an opportunistic approach to host face-to-face, unfiltered, and unstructured conversations with thought leaders from dozens of industries, professions, and community organizations around the world. As we discussed in the Introduction, we believe that this approach has yielded a fresh, new perspective and the opportunity to explore areas of knowledge and perspectives that were nonintuitive and unlikely to have been discovered had we forged a traditional hypothesis.

Whereas these interviews did not start as a science experiment, we screened the data in a thoughtful, four-step process, not so that we could find a prescription, but to discover provocative and useful ideas for readers to consider. The first step was to meet Builders out in the world in an environment where they are normally operating, rather than in a laboratory setting. We sat down with them in their offices, home, or even a hotel room or conferences during their travels. The interview started with an open-ended question, such as "How do you define success?" or "Did you have a plan or did you imagine decades ago where you would be today?" Rather than seeking a particular answer based on a preconceived list of questions, we asked follow-up questions to explore and better understand what the response meant. We then reviewed and screened the interviews by organizational theme codes.

Step 2: Content Analysis— Organizational Theme Codes (OTC)

We identified topic areas, or organization theme codes, that covered the broad landscape of subjects discussed in the interviews. We could have easily found more than 100 categories, or we could have decided on fewer OTCs depending on one's orientation to the data. In the final analysis, we sought to avoid arcane or technical OTCs that would require complex description and instead focused on 21 pragmatic, easy-to-understand themes and their subcategories that often emerge in discussions with management teams, such as leadership, success, risk-taking, failure, and globalization. We filtered the content of the interviews based on those OTCs.

Coding the dialog by these OTCs generated far more ideas than we could cover in a book that we hoped to keep under 300 pages. Those responses that appeared consistently for the majority of the participants and were particularly non-intuitive (to us) were analyzed for the final manuscript. You will notice that many of those insights were also tested in the IdeaMap survey discussed earlier. We hope to revisit and mine further many of these OTCs for future surveys, books, and articles. The following are the OTCs that we used during the interview process:

- **Leadership**—Perspectives, roles, meaning.
- **Risk**—Taking risks, managing risk.
- **Failure**—Harvesting failure, resilience, frequency.
- **Pain**—Grief, lack of fairness, using your pain, managing pain.
- **Confidence**—The role of self-confidence, self-esteem.
- **Focus**—Clarity, letting go, managing time/resources, choosing goals, persistence.
- **Measurability**—Ability to measure goals (both big and small goals).
- **Trust**—Respect, listening, building trust, importance of trust.
- **Values**—The role of core values.
- **Change**—Managing change, helping others through change.
- **Growth**—Encouraging growth, managing it, the need for growth.
- **Excellence/Best**—Doing your best, quality of product.
- **Innovation**—Creativity, how to encourage innovation, giving resources to innovation. The paradox of failure as necessary for innovation.
- **Culture**—Organizational culture; creating a culture around a goal, idea, or passion.
- **Global/Environment**—Globalization, diversity of ideas the environment always wins.
- **Stakeholders**—The role of and relationship with customers, shareholders, community, and suppliers.

- **New Ventures**—The special needs of new ventures, new services, or ideas.
- **Teams**—Managing people; managing yourself, as well as subcategories like the following:
  - **Authority**—Giving power away, holding others accountable, giving resources to the team members. Managing through others.
  - **Skills**—Building other leaders, training, building the team, mentoring.
  - **Rewards/Recognition/Incentives/Gratitude**—Using rewards to focus goals; using rewards to communicate the goals.
  - **Alignment**—With goals/buy-in.
  - **Incentives**—Paying for performance and consequences of ignoring this.
  - **POV**—Communicating the goal and meaning to the team; consistency.
  - **Contention**—Encouraging contention, managing it.
- **Fear**—Managing fear; helping others manage fear.
- **Preparation**—The importance of doing your homework; what's involved in preparation, planning.
- **Passions**—The role of passion; loving your work and life (or not).

Although we were obviously looking for patterns in the personal interviews that might fit into an OTC, we didn't fall into the trap of simply counting the number of occurrences that people uttered one of these things. For example, we would not just listen for the word "fear'" in order for a statement to fall into that section—we would listen to the entire conversation to determine where that idea should be coded. (We found that leaders often deal with or feel fear, but rarely use that word—particularly men!)

If a person we interviewed said "preparation" 23 times, or 3 times as often as other OTCs, then you might jump to the conclusion that she was always prepared or planning, but still not know what role preparation plays in the organization or its relative effectiveness in her strategy. Nor would you know whether any single word translates into actual behavior. In a noble attempt to find a way to code the word "preparation," you could miss the context or the concept that the interviewee was intending. You might even assume, as many authors have, that enduringly successful people had a roadmap that they had prepared or always followed plans that lead them to a preconceived destination. *In fact, Builders almost never said they had imagined at the beginning where they are today.* They thought of preparation as "going deep" into their subject or field or the immediate task that they find is meaningfully engaging to them at that point in their lives. It was a serendipitous journey in which luck favored the prepared.

If a leader used the words "love" and "passion" frequently (and they did in our interviews), we would not just tally the times it was mentioned—we would explore it further to find out more about what those words meant by actually asking him—something you can't do on a survey. Listening to the context made it clearer that leaders were not preaching love in general. Whereas many expressed affection for teammates, employees, and customers, they also were making a very different point during our particular interviews. They insisted to us that *you love your work or you will be beaten by someone else who does.*

Had we simply counted the frequency of a word used in an interview, for example, we also would have missed entirely one of the biggest, most non-intuitive insights in our study: harvesting contention. The word itself was rarely used in the discussions, but Builders incessantly talked about their relationship with their "teams" as if they were playing with their favorite professional ice hockey team. What was rewarding about this interview method was that it provided the space and patience to listen for *their* meaning, not ours, for a change. When you listen for *meaning*, rather than a preset agenda that you have in mind, you get a different picture of what may be going on, and some remarkable insights leap out. In fact, it was surprising to hear the excitement in the voices of leaders over and over again as they described how much they looked forward to spending time with their colleagues—not just for polite collaboration and fellowship, but for sessions that were so creative, productive, and contentious that many Builders said they would be reluctant to allow outsiders witness them.

A written self-assessment or survey has its own value (as we reaffirmed in our success survey), but there is nothing like the experience of meeting someone to discuss issues. We had the good fortune of actually seeing the Builders we interviewed. Whereas people might still attempt to mislead you in person, you have the opportunity to listen and watch for the context and seek samples of behavior as well as the individual words that would lead to placing an idea into an appropriate OTC code.

Step 3: Behavioral Point of View (BPOV)—Archetype Positioning Statements/Identity Narratives

The next step was to take another look at the data and our contextual observations to see how we could frame statements to serve as elements of a survey. In other words, if you could take key traits and narratives that were demonstrated or described during the interviews, what would an archetype of an enduringly successful person say (or not say) about himself or herself in the context of this conversation from a behavioral point of view.

Here are five early samples of narratives from the interviews that later became part of the global study. We reviewed dozens and dozens of statements like these in each OTC, which were used to build the 36 aspects that ultimately formed the *World Success Survey*.

    a. I don't let my (negative) feelings or setbacks hijack the importance of the cause or goal that I'm after.

b. I don't use my mistakes or weaknesses as a reason to distrust my ability. I often think that I learn as much from my failures as my successes.

c. Often the best choices I make use up all the options. Life is rarely a matter of either/or.

d. I don't let what other people think about what I'm doing stop me from doing what I must do.

e. I never could have pictured 20 or 30 years ago where I am today. I earned my luck by loving what I do and making sure I understand everything I can about my field. I never stop learning about it—I can't stop, won't stop; it's who I am. When I'm in doubt, I go deeper and learn more.

Step 4: The World Success Survey

The final step of this process was to launch our second study for this book—a psychographic statistical look at the issues raised in our personal interviews. As described earlier, our Stanford-based team engaged in an additional round of research in association with Pearson/Prentice Hall, Prof. Jerry Wind at The Wharton School at the University of Pennsylvania, and the i-Novation division of Moskowitz Jacobs Inc. (Chuck Loesch, Director of Marketing Research for FiSite Research, also supported the development of this research).

The theoretical foundation of Moskowitz Jacobs Inc.'s work is experimental (statistical) design and mathematical modeling. The technology and software are proprietary, and are based on the work of Dr. Howard Moskowitz, a leading scientist in this field. He holds a Ph.D. in Experimental Psychology (as in the design of statistical experiments and psychophysics) from Harvard University and has written 14 books and more than 300 scientific papers on his innovative work to identify what he calls the "algebra of the consumer mind"—from consumer product innovation and food research, to social issues, health, the stock market, and presidential elections. Moskowitz and a team of researchers worked with us to develop, implement, and evaluate our *World Success Survey* using the IdeaMap conjoint-based computerized concept development technology described earlier.

Exhibit 2

Here is the invitation to participate in World Success Survey, which appeared in the Knowledge@Wharton newsletter:

Leadership and Change
How Successful People Remain Successful

When James C. Collins and Jerry I. Porras wrote their hugely popular 1994 book, *Built to Last: Successful Habits of Visionary Companies*, they began by stating clearly that they did not mean to write about visionary leaders. Their goal was to find visionary companies—the crown jewels of their industries—and discover what made them extraordinary. Then questions arose about the extent to which the principles of *Built to Last* might apply to individuals. That sparked another investigation that has now led to a follow-up book, *Success Built to Last*, which will be published by Wharton School Publishing later this year. Mark Thompson and Stewart Emery, co-authors with Porras of *Success Built to Last*, spoke with Knowledge@Wharton about their book. In addition, the authors are conducting a global survey on how people think about success; a link to the survey can be found at the end of the article.

http://knowledge.wharton.upenn.edu/article/1451.cfm

Exhibit 3

Here are the brief instructions on how to participate in the survey, which appeared when participants clicked on the designated link:

In this section we've constructed a simple 'test'...really a MENU for success.

Please read each menu on the screen. This menu describes a set of aspects of a successful person. Now...how would you feel about this phrase describing a menu for 'lasting success'. Of course, some vignettes will describe success 'almost perfectly', whereas others will be 'far off the mark'.

This survey gives you a chance to help redefine the meaning of lasting success, and ignite a productive dialog about success around the world.

On the following screens, you'll see success menus, one per screen.

Please read each menu as a total idea, and rate the combination on a simple 1-9 scale:

How well does this 'MENU' describe your view of lasting success?

1=Very poorly...9=Very well

As a 'thank you', for your participation, 50 people will be randomly chosen to receive a FREE COPY OF THE BOOK **Success Built to Last: Creating a Life That Matters**.

In addition, we will **send everyone the results of this WORLD SUCCESS SURVEY before it goes to the news media, along with a link to download a free copy of the first chapter of the book and a 50% discount coupon towards the purchase of the book**.

At the end of the interview there are a few more 'classification' questions and then you will be able to see how **your view** of lasting success compares with the views of other participants in the survey.

This WORLD SUCCESS SURVEY should take about 15 minutes.

Please press 'Continue' to start the survey. Just give your 'immediate, gut opinion' of success.

Thank you!

Exhibit 4

Here is an example of the text that would appear on a screen displaying a "menu of success:"

MOTTO...Success means achieving money, fame, or power.

ADVERSITY...I believe that when things go wrong, most people look for a scapegoat.

CAREER...Regardless of what other people think, what motivates me is doing a great job.

VALUES...The main priority in my life is to do meaningful things.

How well does this 'MENU' describe your view of lasting success?	1	2	3	4	5	6	7	8	9
	1=Very poorly...9=Very well								

Exhibit 5

The Regression Model

For those you who enjoy statistics, our method is simple. We begin, for each person, with the combination of ideas (Input 1); i.e., the vignettes or menus. The participant gives us ratings (Input 2). We use simple statistics (regression) to figure out how each individual idea drives the response to the entire success menu.

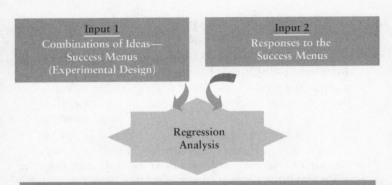

Input 1	Input 2
Combinations of Ideas— Success Menus (Experimental Design)	Responses to the Success Menus

Regression Analysis

Output: *Algebra of the Mind*
The additive model relates the presence/absence of each individual message to the response in terms of describing lasting success.

The additive model for LASTING SUCCESS has these components:

- **Element impact scores (or utility)**—Show you the contribution (conditional probability) of the element to overall "lasting success."

  Positive values indicate that the element *enhances* the likelihood of the perception of success.

  Scores that are *near zero* indicate that the element does not contribute to success.

  Negative values indicate that the element actually *detracts* from success.

- **Additive constant**—Shows you the number of respondents (out of 100) who feel that they are successful, even without a particular element or idea from the Success Menu.

The system also creates groups of like-minded people, who show similar patterns regarding what menu items (elements) they feel describe lasting success. This is the mindset segmentation that we found so informative.

- **No gaming and PC behavior!** Finally, because the IdeaMap system works with menus that change randomly from screen to screen during the interview, it becomes almost impossible to "game the interview" and get away with politically correct answers. Very soon into the interview, the respondent relaxes, and gives a fast and honest "gut reaction." The answers come out blazingly quickly as the respondent reacts in a normal everyday manner, soon dropping the standard defenses that so often defeat standard surveys.

Exhibit 6

Impact Scores for the World Survey

Regression analysis (see Exhibit 5) relating the rating responses to the test stimuli (our "menus of success") show the contribution (positive or negative) for each of the aspects of success in our survey. These scores are the basis for measuring the absolute impact of each aspect of success and comparing that impact to all the others. The result is a wide range of scores across the success aspects in this research. On the table below you can see we have reported the responses for the three attitudinal segments in the survey from a high of +21, indicating a very positive relation to success, to a low of –28, indicating a very negative relation. (Our experience suggests that, for this research, scores of +6 or higher and –6 or lower are identifying important and notable results.) Such a wide range of scores underscores the strongly-held feelings being expressed by the respondents, and allows us a clear reading of these feelings. As a sample of the findings, we have provided below a broad comparison of the differences of everyone in the three attitudinal segments. This is just one of many ways to slice and dice this fascinating data.

	Meaning—Segment 1	ThoughtStyle—Segment 2	ActionStyle—Segment 3
Base Size	160	105	99
Constant	36	40	41
MOTTO...Success means I can make a difference and create lasting impact.	17	8	12
VALUES...The main priority in my life is to do meaningful things.	9	12	6
MOTTO...Success means I am engaged in a life of personal fulfillment.	12	7	6
BALANCE...Balance to me is spending the RIGHT amounts of time on work, family, personal interests, and community.	4	21	3
MOTTO...Success means I have the freedom to do what is meaningful.	9	8	2
MOTTO...Success means I create strong relationships and connections with people.	6	7	3
ADVERSITY...I learn more from my failures than I learn from my successes.	7	10	-3
ADVERSITY...Setbacks don't make me ABANDON my passions or causes.	10	5	2
CAREER...It is absolutely necessary for me to work in a job that I really love.	-2	-1	15
MOTTO...Success means I am happy.	3	1	8
LEADERSHIP...Success comes from setting big goals in both my personal life and my professional life.	11	-7	3
CAREER...Regardless of what other people think, what motivates me most is doing a great job.	-5	10	12
VALUES...I'm most successful when my team shares my values.	2	2	7

	Meaning—Segment 1	ThoughtStyle—Segment 2	ActionStyle—Segment 3
LEADERSHIP...It's essential to me to encourage people to share views that disagree with my own views.	14	–8	9
VALUES...I believe there is one clear set of values to guide my life's choices.	2	–3	3
PASSIONS...Pursuing many different passions increases my effectiveness and creativity.	1	12	2
ADVERSITY...It's painful to me not to do something that is meaningful.	7	4	–7
PASSIONS...People who count support me in following my passions.	4	2	2
LEADERSHIP...Whatever I'm doing I make sure to be good at it.	7	–6	7
ADVERSITY...Setbacks don't make me QUESTION my passions or causes.	6	3	–10
BALANCE...I need a long-term relationship in my personal life for lasting success.	–5	6	–10
LEADERSHIP...To accomplish what matters to me, it may be necessary to go against the wishes of people who count.	3	–11	8
LEADERSHIP...My boss supports what I believe to be meaningful and important.	9	–14	1
BALANCE...Balance to me is spending EQUAL amounts of time on work, family, personal interests, and community.	–8	1	–12
ADVERSITY...Sometimes it's disappointing to achieve a goal and discover that it has little meaning to me.	–2	–2	–21
VALUES...When I have a major change in my life, it helps to reconsider and then change some of my values.	–7	–5	–2

	Meaning— Segment 1	ThoughtStyle— Segment 2	ActionStyle— Segment 3
CAREER...It's always been clear to me what I wanted to do for the rest of my life.	-22	-11	-6
LEADERSHIP...I don't share all my doubts, judgments, and concern(s) with my team because it is more important to say what is appropriate to achieve our goals, even at the loss of some authenticity.	-5	-19	-14
VALUES...There is one passion—"just one big thing"—that guides my life.	-10	-9	-12
CAREER...It would be nice but not necessarily practical to work in a job that I really love.	-19	-9	-5
VALUES...I believe that most people in business are driven by attaining fame, money, or power.	-11	-14	-20
BALANCE...I prefer to pursue one of two alternatives rather than trying to make both work.	-16	-3	-14
MOTTO...Success means I am achieving fame, money, or power.	-11	-21	-19
CAREER...My career has followed a precise roadmap that I myself created.	-18	-24	-6
ADVERSITY...I believe that when things go wrong, most people look for a scapegoat.	-10	-10	-20
CAREER...To stay on track with my goals, it's best to rely on the opinions of others.	-28	-18	-14

E N D N O T E S

Introduction

1. Collins, James C., and Jerry I. Porras. *Built to Last*. New York, NY: HarperCollins, 2002.

2. See "Biographical Index" for a list of interviewees included in this book.

3. Kosman, Joshua. "Innovators of Our Time, Smithsonian magazine's 35 who made a difference." *Smithsonian Magazine*, 36:8 (November 2005): 87–88.

4. See "The Pleasure of Finding Things Out—A Look at the Research Behind *Success Built to Last*."

Chapter 1

1. *Encarta World English Dictionary*, ed. Anne Soukhanov. (New York, NY: St.Martin's Press, 1999) s.v. "success."

2. Wipro Limited. 2006. "Azim H. Premji." *About Wipro*. http://www.wipro.com/aboutus/azim_profile.htm.

3. Alice Waters is a strong advocate for farmer's markets and for sound and sustainable agriculture. In 1996, celebrating Chez Panisse's 25th anniversary, she created the Chez Panisse Foundation to help underwrite cultural and educational programs, such as the one at the *Edible Schoolyard*.

4. Red, green, and blue are the additive primary colors, and produce white when combined. Yellow, cyan, and magenta are the subtractive primary colors, and produce black when combined. (Annenberg Media. 1997–2006. "Primary Colors." *Workshop 3*. http:// www.learner.org/channel/workshops/sheddinglight/ highlights/highlights3.html.)

5. Tarrant, John J. *Drucker: The Man Who Invented the Corporate Society.* New York, NY: Van Nostrand Reinhold, 1976.

6. Brigman, June, and Mary Schmich. "Brenda Starr." Tribune Media Services, http://www.comicspage.com/ brendastarr/brenda_characters.html.

Chapter 2

1. (Sparrow, 1998). Niven, David. *100 Simple Secrets of Successful People.* New York, NY: HarperCollins, 2002.

2. Researchers offering money in exchange for creative solutions to problems find that monetary rewards are unrelated to people's capacity to offer original ideas. Instead, creativity is more frequently the product of genuine interest in the problem and a belief that superiors appreciate creativity (Cooper, Clasen, Silva-Jaleonen, and Butler, 1999). Niven, David.
100 Simple Secrets of Successful People. New York, NY: HarperCollins, 2002.

3. Girl Scouts of the United States of America. 1998–2005. *Who We Are.* http://www.girlscouts.org/ who-we-are/.

4. Leader to Leader Institute. 2006. "Frances Hesselbein Biography." *About the Institute.* http://www.pfdf.org/ about/fh-bio.html.

5. Csikszentmihalyi, Mihaly. *Flow: The Psychology of Optimal Experience.* New York, NY: HarperCollins, 1990.

Chapter 3

1. Born Marguerite Ann Johnson, she received the name Maya Angelou in her twenties after debuting as a dancer at the Purple Onion cabaret.

2. Angelou, Maya. *I Know Why the Caged Bird Sings.* New York, NY: Random House, 1969.

3. She holds the lifetime chair as Z. Smith Reynolds Professor of American Studies at Wake Forest University.

4. Seven out of 10 corporate leaders who survive longest in their jobs downplay both the best and worst outcomes they experienced. When asked what they attribute to their successes and failures, people are seven times as likely to focus on effort when describing a success as they are when describing a failure. This tendency is 19% greater among inexperienced workers, who take even more credit for success and dish out blame for

failures—learning nothing in the process (Moeller and Koeller, 2000.) Niven, David. *100 Simple Secrets of Successful People*. New York, NY: HarperCollins, 2002.

5. Ibarra, Herminia. "How to Stay Stuck in the Wrong Career." *Harvard Business Review* (December 2002): 40.

6. Brown, Jeffrey, Sandeep Junnarkar, Mukul Pandya, Robbie Shell, and Susan Warner. *Nightly Business Report Presents Lasting Leadership*. Upper Saddle River, NJ: Wharton School Publishing, 2005.

7. Bono and Bill Gates. Press conference, World Economic Forum, New York, NY, February 3, 2002.

8. Bono Quotes from an interview with the World Association of Newspapers for World Press Freedom Day in May 2004. http://www.reference.com/browse/ wiki/Bono.

Chapter 4

1. Collins, James C., and Jerry I. Porras. *Built to Last*, pp. 222. New York: HarperCollins, 2002.

2. Ibid.

3. Collins, James C., and Jerry I. Porras. *Built to Last*, pp.229. New York: HarperCollins, 2002.

4. Bloom, Harold. "Heroes and Icons: Billy Graham." *Time*, June 14, 1999, www.Time.com/time/time100/ heroes/profile/graham01.html.

Chapter 5

1. Penguin Group (USA), Inc. 2004. "Tom Clancy." *Tom Clancy*. http://us.penguingroup.com/static/packages/us/ tomclancy/bio.html.

2. Naval Institute Press originally published this novel. It is the first work of fiction they ever published and it is still the most successful. Clancy, Tom. *The Hunt for Red October*. Annapolis, MD: Naval Institute Press, 1984.

3. Ibarra, Herminia. "How to Stay Stuck in the Wrong Career." *Harvard Business Review* (December 2002): pp. 40–47.

4. Patagonia, Inc. 2006. "Company History." *Company Info*. http://www.patagonia.com.

5. Waxman, Sharon. "The Oscar Acceptance Speech: By and Large It's a Lost Art." *Washington Post*, March 21, 1999, http://www.littlereview.com/goddesslouise/articles/oscrpost.htm.

6. Collins, James C., and Jerry I. Porras. *Built to Last*. New York, NY: HarperCollins, 2002.

7. See "The Pleasure of Finding Things Out—A Look at the Research Behind *Success Built to Last*."

8. Commencement address by Steve Jobs, CEO of Apple Computer and of Pixar Animation Studios, June 12, 2005, http://news-service.stanford.edu/news/2005/june15/jobs-061505.html.

Chapter 6

1. The Gorilla Foundation. 2003. "Penny Patterson, Ph.D.: President and Director of Research." *The Foundation*. http://www.koko.org/foundation/ penny.html.

2. Sixty-eight percent of people who consider themselves a success say there is at least one area of their jobs at which they are an expert (Austin, 2000). Niven, David. *100 Simple Secrets of Successful People*. New York, NY: HarperCollins, 2002.

3. Russakoff, Dale. "Lessons of Might and Right." *Washington Post Magazine,* September 9, 2001, W23, www.washingtonpost.com/wp-dyn/articles/ A54664-2001Sep6.html.

   Hoover Institution: Stanford University. 2006. "Condoleezza Rice: Thomas and Barbara Stephenson Senior Fellow." *Hoover Institution*. www.hoover.org/bios/rice.html.

   The White House. "Condoleezza Rice, Secretary of State." *The White House*. www.whitehouse.gov/government/ rice-bio.html.

   Manafian, Lisa. "Power from Within." *The Black Perspective*, November 19, 2004, http://www.blackperspective.com/pages/ mag_articles/spring2002_rice.html.

4. Kettmann, Steve. "Bush's Secret Weapon." *Salon.com*, March 20, 2000, http://dir.salon.com/story/ politics2000/feature/2000/03/20/rice/index.html.

5. Iowa State University's Brad Bushman and Case Western University's Roy Baumeister learned that high self-confidence is as likely—or is perhaps more likely—to appear in sociopaths as it is to appear in those with low self-esteem. Goode, Erica. "Deflating Self-Esteem's Role in Society's Ills." *New York Times,* October 1,

2002, http://query.nytimes.com/gst/
fullpage.html?sec=health&res=9A02EEDA1538F932A35753C1A9
649C8B63.

Self-esteem, by itself, does not predict success. In fact, those with particularly high self-esteem are 26% more vulnerable to the consequences of failures and setbacks because of the devastating effect negative outcomes can have on their self-image (Coover and Murphy, 2000). Niven, David. *100 Simple Secrets of Successful People*. New York, NY: HarperCollins, 2002.

Chapter 7

1. Enberg, Dick. *Humorous Quotes for All Occasions*. Kansas City, MO: Andrews McMeel, 2000.

2. Among managers in upper-level positions, 84% report having had to deal with a "period of discomfort" in their lives. Some took career risks, worked for long hours, or acquired new skills, but they say the sacrifice is necessary to pursue employment, promotion, and success (Atkinson, 1999). Of people who feel they have failed to achieve success, 64% point to a specific standard others have set that they were unable to live up to (Arnold, 1995). Niven, David. *100 Simple Secrets of Successful People*. New York, NY: HarperCollins, 2002.

Chapter 8

1. The first definition listed in the *Merriam-Webster Online Dictionary* doesn't quite capture our point; please see the second definition. "1: the imaginative projection of a subjective state into an object so that the object appears to be infused with it 2: the action of understanding, being aware of, being sensitive to, and vicariously experiencing the feelings, thoughts, and experience of another of either the past or present without having the feelings, thoughts, and experience fully communicated in an objectively explicit manner." Merriam-Webster. 2005–2006. "empathy." *Merriam-Webster Online Dictionary*. http://www.m-w.com/dictionary/empathy.

2. Murty, L.S., and Janat Shah. "Compassionate, High Quality Health Care at Low Cost: The Aravind Model," interview with Dr. G. Venkataswamy and R.D. Thulasiraj, *IIMB Management Review*, September 2004, http://www.aravind.org/downloads/IIMB.pdf.

3. Huntsman, Jon M. *Winners Never Cheat*, pp. 113. Upper Saddle River, NJ: Wharton School Publishing, 2005.

4. According to Joe Nichols, that section of roadway was later reengineered and rebuilt because traffic overburdened it and, apparently, the turn contributed to other accidents. In the meantime, Joe has rebuilt his life. When the town settled out of court for $75,000, Joe put that modest nest egg to work in his company.

Chapter 9

1. The American Heritage Dictionary of the English Language, 4th ed. "serendipity." *The American Heritage Dictionary of the English Language*, 4th ed. www.bartleby.com/61/93/S0279300.html.

2. Remer, Theodore G., ed., with Introduction and Notes. *Serendipity and The Three Princes: From the Peregrinaggio of 1557*. Norman, OK: University of Oklahoma Press, 1965.

   Merton, Robert K., and Elinor Barber. *The Travels and Adventures of Serendipity: A Study in Sociological Semantics and the Sociology of Science*. Princeton, NJ: Princeton University Press, 2004.

3. Collins, James C., and Jerry I. Porras. *Built to Last*, pp. 94. New York, NY: HarperCollins, 2002.

4. Ibid.

5. Rosten, Leo. *The Joys of Yiddish*. Pocket Books, 2000.

6. Collins, James C., and Jerry I. Porras. *Built to Last*, pp.105. New York, NY: HarperCollins, 2002.

7. Brown, Jeffrey, Sandeep Junnarkar, Mukul Pandya, Robbie Shell, and Susan Warner. *Nightly Business Report Presents Lasting Leadership*. Upper Saddle River, NJ: Wharton School Publishing, 2005.

Chapter 10

1. Leadership consultant Jim Moore hosts sessions in which an organization's values and mission statement are put on mock trial. One set of managers handles the defense and another set prosecutes, as if in a court of law. This is an engaging and useful way to give full permission to push on politically incorrect issues that might otherwise be sacrosanct. It also is a highly effective approach for arbitrating simmering disputes that might not otherwise get a fair hearing.

Chapter 11

1. Focus: HOPE. "Eleanor M. Josaitis," *About Focus: HOPE.* http://www.focushope.edu/about.htm#josaitis.

2. Napoleon Hill (October 26, 1883–November 8, 1970) was one of the earliest American authors of personal-success literature. His most famous work, *Think and Grow Rich*, is one of the best-selling books of all time. Hill, Napolean. *Think and Grow Rich*. New York, NY: Fawcett Books, 1960.

3. Self-motivated people, who feel they control their own lives, are hardier and more resilient than people who feel external forces control them. Siebert, Al. *The Resiliency Advantage*. San Francisco, CA: Berrett-Koehler Publishers, 2005.

The Pleasure of Finding Things Out— A Look at the Research Behind Success Built to Last

1. Feynman, Richard P., et al. *The Pleasure of Finding Things Out: The Best Short Works of Richard P. Feynman*. New York, NY: Perseus Books, 1999.

2. The metaphor that Collins and Porras used in thinking about how to select the comparison companies in the *Built to Last* study was one of a horse race. Two horses started the race at the same time (founding date) in the same place (industry) for the same length of time (until 1990). The basic question that could then be asked is, "What did the Visionary horse do in running the race that the Comparison horse did not do?" To use that comparison in the context of a company was fine for *Built to Last*, but for an individual person, it quickly becomes problematic. The birthdate of the person could be parallel to the founding date of an organization (or horse). But what is the parallel to industry? Is it education, profession, company, organization affiliation, or dozens of other possible factors? How do we identify the comparison person based on their not having achieved the same level of success as the enduringly successful people in our study? Do we pick "losers?" Do we pick an individual who is not quite as successful? How do we determine that? In *Built to Last*, we did not use success as a key factor for picking the comparison companies. Differences in performance of the two groups of companies in the *Built to Last* research were discovered after the selection of the companies, not before. Enduringly successful people might look like race horses, but they believe their success would have been undermined had they been fixated on competition for the decades

in which they had achieved so highly. As it turns out, one of the most significant findings in the two studies upon which *Success Built to Last* is constructed is that only an individual can define for herself or himself the criteria for success based on their own sense of what it means—and that the traditional measures of achievement, fame, wealth, and power were outcomes from years of effort, not the driving factors in the belief systems of enduringly successful people!

BIOGRAPHICAL INDEX

We are grateful for the opportunity to continue to meet so many fascinating people. The following summary includes many individuals we've interviewed to-date, but not those who participated in our quantitative study, *World Success Survey*. As we've noted throughout this manuscript, our interviewees were not selected to create an "honor roll" list that we're offering to you as role models for success. (There are plenty of media and other organizations that are in the business of making those judgments, and we relied on them to find many of these interesting folks.) We wanted to learn what people who have had 20+ years of impact on their fields of endeavor had in common. One of the most poignant lessons they provided was that you can't rely on role models—you must choose your own definition of success, rather than assume you need someone else's by default or envy. We look forward to hearing your stories, your research, and your suggestions about people we should meet to expand this conversation at www.SuccessBuiltToLast.com.

[†] Our interview with this individual is included in our study and influenced this manuscript, but we didn't have room to fit everyone's insightful stories. We list the interviewees here as an example of the eclectic collection of successful people we were grateful to meet.

INDEX

271